OLD WAYS, OLD SECRETS

OLD WAYS, OLD SECRETS

PAGAN IRELAND:
FROM ANCIENT MYTH TO MODERN TRADITION

JO KERRIGAN

PHOTOGRAPHY BY **RICHARD MILLS**

FALL RIVER PRESS

New York

FALL RIVER PRESS

New York

An Imprint of Sterling Publishing Co., Inc.
1166 Avenue of the Americas
New York, NY 10036

This 2017 edition published by Fall River Press by arrangement with The O'Brien Press.

ISBN 978-1-4351-6553-3

For information about custom editions, special sales, and premium
and corporate purchases, please contact Sterling Special Sales at
800-805-5489 or specialsales@sterlingpublishing.com.

Manufactured in the United States of America

2 4 6 8 10 9 7 5 3 1

www.sterlingpublishing.com

Cover design by Elizabeth Lindy

In Ireland, the Otherworld and its spirits are taken for granted. Wherever you go, you will find evidence of ancient beliefs, customs and traditions.

Contents

Part Two: *Nature and the Otherworld*
SACRED PLACES, MAGICAL CREATURES AND THE TURNING YEAR

Part Three: *Traditions in Story*
THE THREE SORROWS OF STORYTELLING

Introduction

Living in West Cork, and having travelled through every corner of Ireland, I am always struck by the natural way in which the Otherworld and its spirits are taken for granted. Wherever you go, you will find evidence of ancient beliefs, customs and traditions that continue to this day. Why do we still observe practices whose origin and purpose we have completely forgotten?

Or have we? Do the people of Ireland still, deep in the subconscious, retain beliefs that were already old when Christianity arrived on these shores? Do we still instinctively reach towards a time when nature and the cycle of the seasons were of paramount importance, and the spirits that governed the circle of the year were honoured as they should be?

In this book, I have presented evidence that the old ways are still very much with us. Festivals celebrated with great energy and enthusiasm may now bear the name of various saints, but they can be traced back to celebrations honouring older gods or goddesses. Pilgrimages to high mountains or remote lake islands once had far more to do with druids and oracles than with Christian observances.

All you have to do is lift the bright modern overlay, just a little, and peep underneath. You will find the old ways and the old beliefs are still there, as strong as ever. Come and explore. This book will start you on a journey. How far you travel is up to you.

Lift the bright modern overlay, just a little, and peep underneath. The old ways and the old beliefs are still there, as strong as ever.

So Many Came: A Historical Overview

Over thousands of years, many different peoples have sought Ireland's green land and gentle climate. Legend, folk memory and imagination are inextricably tangled with fact in texts such as the *Leabhar Gabhála* (*Book of Invasions*). The following is a rough chronology, which may be useful as a basic guide to our history of settlement.

Over thousands of years, many different peoples have sought Ireland's fertile land and gentle climate.

AFTER THE FLOOD

According to the *Leabhar Gabhála*, Ireland's first inhabitants were led by Parthalon, arriving from Greece about 300 years after the Deluge, and landing at the mouth of the Kenmare River in Kerry. Another 300 years later, it tells us that 9,000 of his people died in a single week on Sean Mhagh Ealta Edair (modern Tallaght in Dublin). Tellingly, the old name for Tallaght translates as the 'Plain of the Plague', adding strength to this brief record of a long-ago calamity.

Following this virtual wipeout of Parthalon's descendants, Ireland was apparently left empty for 30 years. Perhaps the story of disease and sudden death spread along the seaways, and it was avoided. But then, from Scythia on the borders of Europe and Asia, came Nemed and his sons. If they were hoping for peace and quiet in their new home, however, they didn't get it. Soon after their arrival, the Nemedians were attacked by a particularly unpleasant band known as the Fomorians, who counted the terrifying Balor of the Evil Eye among their number. Balor, a kind of weapon of mass destruction who echoed the death-dealing abilities of the Greek Medusa, had only to look upon someone to kill instantaneously.

The Fomorians appear to have been sea pirates rather than settlers, descending on Ireland at regular intervals to loot and demand protection money. Legend suggests that they had an outpost on Tory Island off Donegal. Possibly early Norsemen, the Fomorians are the baddies of Irish legendary history, reappearing at intervals to create panic and havoc throughout several waves of settlers.

Discouraged by the rapacious demands of the Fomorians, the surviving Nemedians, we are told, emigrated in three separate directions: one group to northern Europe, one to Greece, and one to the neighbouring island of Britain. First to return was the Grecian group, who again settled Ireland and became known as the Fir Bolg, or Bag Men, from their sensible habit of carrying good, rich earth in woven bags wherever they went, so that they could be sure of making the land fertile. Small, dark, gentle farming folk, they cared for the land and worshipped the spirits of nature who made the rain fall, the sun shine, and the crops grow.

THE PEOPLE OF DANU

The Nemedians who had gone to the northern lands had spent their time perfecting the arts of divination, druidism and philosophy. (This does suggest that, even back in earliest times, such craft was known to be taught in the far North, in Scandinavia, perhaps even in Russia.) A couple of centuries later, these emigrants came back as the skilled, wise and powerful Tuatha Dé Danann, or people of Danu, the great earth goddess. Powerful in the arts of magic, they easily overcame the unwarlike Fir Bolg.

The time of the Tuatha Dé Danann in Ireland was a golden age of beauty and joy.

The time of the Tuatha Dé Danann in Ireland was a golden age of beauty and joy, music and song. Kind and generous, these tall, fair-haired people did not drive out the Fir Bolg after taking over but left them in peace to tend their crops and herds in their own remote forests and boglands. And it is the Tuatha Dé Danann who put the Fomorians out of the picture once and for all by slaying Balor of the Evil Eye.

But yet another invader was preparing to cross the sea to Ireland, this time from the south. The Celts, wandering westward across Europe for many thousands of years, had long believed that their destiny lay in green Inisfáil, the island on the edge of the world. They finally made the voyage from the coast of northern Spain, with battleships and warriors, prepared to drive out whoever already lived in this land of plenty and seize it for themselves, for the Celts were a warlike people, always ready to fight for honour and glory as well as material gain.

With them came a new attitude, in which battle skills and personal honour were regarded as more important than anything else. Their gods, both male and female, were more likely to drive a battle chariot than to ensure a bountiful crop, and it is at this time that the cult of the half-god hero-warrior, exemplified in Cúchulainn, comes to the fore, and essentially male qualities take priority over female ones.

The Celts fought ferociously for what they saw as their promised land and, to stop the bloodshed that they deplored, the Tuatha Dé Danann yielded. But, the legends assert firmly, they did not leave. They loved Ireland and cared for it far too much. Instead, they withdrew gracefully and mysteriously into the very land itself, taking up their new habitations in grassy mounds and ancient hills, beneath thorn trees and stone circles. Here, immortal, they live still, in splendid palaces amid wonderful gardens and enchanted forests, and their music and song continues as before.

Occasionally, usually at the time of the great natural divisions of the year, such as the Celtic festivals of Bealtaine and Samhain, they ride forth once more across the land that was theirs, and mingle with the human beings. The great heroes of Irish legend often have some Tuatha Dé Danann blood in their veins, and their birth may be the result of a chance meeting between a young man or woman from this world and a bright figure from the Otherworld. Many are the stories of unsuspecting men, women and children, coaxed by a beautiful princess or handsome prince to come away to Tír na nÓg, the Land of Youth. A wonderful world awaits those who go, but their chances of returning are slight.

The *Leabhar Gabhála* is a fascinating document because, underneath the decorative layers of storytelling and old legends – and the inevitable Biblical interpolations from Christian scribes – can be found the true gold seam of genuine bardic and oral memory, of real events from history. All legends possess this kernel of truth at their centre. The challenge is to submerge yourself in the wealth of poetic metaphor and discern a hint of the truth – of who came from where, who succeeded them, and what might have happened next.

Because, of course, something always happens next. Though the *Leabhar Gabhála* ends with the coming of the Celts, we are by this time in the realm of recorded events, and life in Ireland continued to create history.

THE COMING OF CHRISTIANITY

After the Celts, another wave of invaders came from the East. This time, they were proponents of the new Christian religion from Rome. Although few in number, their determination to capture Ireland for their own was strong. That they succeeded so well was due to a practical outlook by the first missionaries.

Perceiving that the old ways and old beliefs were immovably entrenched, they simply blended their own doctrines into these, here giving a new name to an old spirit, and there attributing a heroic event to a Christian saint rather than a pagan warrior. And so the people of Ireland combined the new ways with the old, and continued to seek aid from a sacred well or give due reverence to a powerful goddess at her shrine, not bothering too much that the names had changed.

Then came the Norsemen, searching first for plunder and slaves, and later settling to put their knowledge of seafaring and trading to use in the coastal cities they founded at Cork, Dublin, Limerick and Waterford. Although viewed with horror by the Christian monks (who, to be fair, were usually on the receiving end of their raids), the Norse beliefs, in fact, blended easily with those of earlier Ireland. The Norse Otherworld tends to be darker and more menacing than the Celtic, but Irish leprechauns are cousins to Scandinavian elves, and the Mórrígan, the Celtic goddess of battle, sister to the Valkyrie daughters of Odin.

Later still, and England casts covetous and nervous eyes on its near neighbour. Covetous because they could make good use of Ireland's plentiful timber, crops and cattle; nervous because sea access from France and Spain was all too easy, and Ireland was sympathetic to both these southern countries. On the first wave of Norman English settlers, in the 12th century, Ireland worked her magic once more: they became, as the famous phrase has it, 'more Irish than the Irish themselves'.

The second wave, in the 16th and 17th centuries, imposed a harsher rule. Ulster in particular, which had been the most powerful of Irish provinces, had its native nobility deprived of their land and titles (leading to a tragic forced exodus in 1607 that became known as the Flight of the Earls) and was transformed into a settled, English-ruled land. Interestingly, a similar attempt at large-scale settlement in Cork, in the far south, largely failed, the settlers either abandoning their lands or becoming absorbed into local culture. Perhaps being further away from the watchful eye of London had something to do with it?

As before, the people of Ireland proved resilient and adaptable. By now forbidden to practise their Catholic religion, they simply continued in secret, often returning to do so at the old stones, circles and rocks where they had worshipped as pagans for thousands of years. Charged to speak only English and not their native tongue, they treasured the old stories and songs even more, passing them from one generation to the next.

And so it continues. Today's invaders are more likely to descend from a tour bus than a boat, carry guidebooks and cameras rather than a broadsword, shield or crucifix. But they still seek something that only Ireland can give, something that it has retained beneath its modern layers, something that is there for the taking, for all those that have eyes to see. And like their predecessors over thousands of years, they, too, will be changed.

The people of Ireland combined the new ways with the old, not bothering too much that the names had changed.

St Gobnait's well and penal mass rock in Co. Cork.

Part One

The Keepers of Power

DRUIDS, DEITIES AND SUPERHEROES

The druids of ancient Ireland were
all-powerful and treated with reverence.

Druids: Guardians of Wisdom

Healers blending miraculous herbal cures, and advisers sending secret messages in code. Bards reciting the proud genealogies of high kings, and poets composing scathing satires. Shadowy figures murmuring incantations in the forest, and augurers prophesying the future. Brehons explaining the complexities of the ancient laws, and fearsome figures driving war chariots through the battlefield. The druids of ancient Ireland did all this and more; they were mysterious, powerful and treated with reverence – even by those who wore a crown.

WHO WERE THE DRUIDS?

Druids were not rulers or priests in the way we would understand such roles today. They did not dictate or enforce. They were, rather, the repository of knowledge, the guardians of laws, genealogies, history, herbal healing, tree lore, and the epic tales of heroic events. They carried this knowledge in their heads, and their communities relied on their prodigious memories.

They were guides and advisers, and were at the heart of any political intrigue. Above all, the druids were that vital link with the Otherworld; beings who could pass between both realities, who could seek answers from the gods, beg a boon, influence the Fates, or even shape-change at will. As such, they were regarded as the most important people in the land. Free of the obligation to pay taxes or do fighting service, they sat at the king's high table and were deferred to. Those who were not attached to a royal household but maintained their own schools were sought after for cures and spells, and to answer questions in desperate times.

DRUIDS IN LEGEND

The central role of druids in Irish culture is evident from earliest sources, and they are woven into a thousand legends. Parthalon, one of our earliest settlers, brought three of these wise advisers with him, named as Fios, Eolus and Fochmarc; that is, Intelligence, Knowledge and Inquiry.

The Fir Bolg had their own druids too, Cesard being the chief of them. Dian Cecht was a great healer druid of the Tuatha Dé Danann. Cathbad was the most venerated adviser of King Conor Mac Nessa's court in Ulster. Ciothruadh, the oldest and wisest of King Cormac Mac Airt's druids, could raise powerful spells to aid the king in battle. Finegas was the ancient sage and druid living by the River Boyne to whom Fionn Mac Cumhaill went to study poetry and wisdom, while Fear Doirche was the evil druid who turned Fionn's great love, Sadbh, into a deer. In *The Voyage of Mael Duin*, Nuca is the wise wizard who not only counsels the hero on the exact day to begin building his boat, but also the precise number of people he should take with him.

The druids' status could backfire on them. In the *Táin Bó Cúailnge* (*The Cattle Raid of Cooley*), when Maeve's army was on the march, several druids came out from Ossory to welcome it but were attacked in the belief that they were spies:

> And the soldiers set to hunting them until they fled with great speed in the form of deer, into the stones at Liac Mor in the north, for they were wizards of great cunning.

DRUIDS AND THE TUATHA DÉ DANANN

The Tuatha Dé Danann are said to have learned their occult skills from four great druids in the northern lands – Morfesa, Esras, Semias and Uiscias – and brought many more, both male and female, when they returned to Ireland. It was three of their druidesses who caused clouds of darkness and mist to envelop the Fir Bolg while they were holding a council of war, and thus defeated them. The Dé Danann, however, were themselves vanquished by druidic practices from the invading Celts, which is how they came to leave the visible landscape and create their own magical Otherworld underneath the hills and fairy forts, where they still live today.

This, so the old stories say, is how it happened. The Celts, travelling from Galicia in modern-day Spain, made landfall on the Kerry

coast and marched immediately on Tara. The rulers argued that they had been unfairly taken by surprise and requested that the invaders withdraw in their boats 'beyond the Ninth Wave' from Ireland's shores. If they should then succeed in landing once more, the sovereignty of the land would be surrendered to them. Of course as soon as the Celts were beyond the magical 'Ninth Wave' (where it is deemed you are outside the boundaries of Ireland), the druids of the Dé Danann caused a thick mist to rise, concealing the land completely. At the same time they raised a ferocious tempest, scattering the ships of their enemy far and wide.

However, Amergin, poet and druid of the invading host, knew a few spells of his own and, standing on the prow of his wildly tossing boat, he pronounced a powerful declamation that lifted the mist, calmed the storm, turned the tide, and enabled the Celts to gain the land once more. That declamation survives, a very early poem indeed, with possibly some genuine druidical chanting within its lines:

I pray that we reach the land of Erinn, we who are riding
upon the great, productive, vast sea.
That we be distributed upon her plains, her mountains, and

her valleys; upon her forests that shed showers of nuts and all other fruits; upon her rivers and her cataracts; upon her lakes and her great waters; upon her abounding springs.

That we may hold our fairs and equestrian sports upon her territories.

That there may be a king from us in Tara; and that Tara be the territory of our many kings.

That the sons of Milesius be manifestly seen upon her territories.

That noble Erinn be the home of the ships and boats of the sons of Milesius.

Erinn which is now in darkness, it is for her that this oration is pronounced.

The druids of the Dé Danann would conjure a mist to confuse their enemies.

Manipulating the weather was a druidical skill, especially the calling down of dense fogs or magical mists for various purposes: so that their own people could pass safely through enemy territory, or so that an advancing army would become confused and unable to fight. In the *Táin*, a battle mist hid the advancing Ulster army from the men of Connacht, while in the Fenian Cycle, the druid Tadgh used fog to prevent Cumhall, father of Fionn, from finding his magic weapons. Even today you will find country folk saying of the grey rain clouds drifting over the hills that 'the druids are passing'.

FORETELLING THE FUTURE

In times of peace, having enough rain to moisten the soil or enough sun to ripen the crops was a constant worry, and druids were much in demand. Whether they could guarantee the right conditions is arguable, but they knew how to read the weather signs and foretell extreme conditions. It is a talent most of us could develop to some degree if we took the time to observe wind direction, cloud formation and, of course, animal behaviour.

In times of war, it did not do to embark on any great enterprise without first consulting the druids. In the *Táin*, when the armies of Connacht are assembling for the great raid on Ulster, they are held back until the most auspicious moment:

> *Then the four provinces of Ireland were assembled until they were in Cruachan Ai. And their poets and their druids would not let them go thence till the end of a fortnight, waiting for a good omen.*

Druids were conscious of the earth itself as a living being. They were also well versed in the knowledge of the skies, the stars and the moon, and could advise on the best time to undertake a particular task, or to put seeds into the ground as the moon waxed or waned. Today, many wise old country folk retain and use this commonsense knowledge for planting crops or pruning fruit trees.

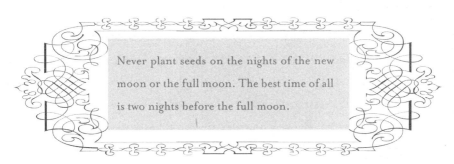

Never plant seeds on the nights of the new moon or the full moon. The best time of all is two nights before the full moon.

Druids answered the questions of kings – Will my sons hold the crown after me? Should we ally with this neighbouring chieftain or make war on him? – but ordinary, everyday people in ancient times had their concerns too. What does life hold for me? What path should I follow? How do I make this person love me? Can I trust this friend's advice? It is part of human nature to seek answers, to pierce the mysterious unknown that lies ahead.

THE LORE OF TREES

It is in keeping with a nature-based religion that Irish druids should use trees for the purpose of divination. With their great roots reaching deep into the earth, their arms opening to the heavens and their heads near the sky, these natural symbols of life itself were sacred, and reverenced as such by all druids, who recognised their importance in the general good health of the world.

Even the unique ogham alphabet used by the druids was linked to individual trees, each letter representing a specific species. Spirits of the Otherworld were held to inhabit trees; to damage one knowingly was to invite ill fortune. Every settlement had its own *bile* or sacred tree under which all ceremonials were conducted.

Old legends speak of the Five Great Trees of Ireland, which held the safety of the land in their keeping. Tortu, an ash, and Mugna, an oak, grew in Meath; Uisneach and the Tree of Dathe, both ash, in Westmeath; and the Tree of Ross, a yew, grew in Co. Carlow. The last-named, however, may well have originated in an ancient forest far to the southwest that still survives today. In an account of the creation of Tara, the seer Fintan, said to have lived in Ireland since the Deluge, recalls:

Rocks bearing traces of ogham, a unique early writing system, are found in prehistoric sites all over Ireland, such as Rathcroghan in Co. Roscommon.

One day I passed through a wood of West Munster in the west. I took away with me a red yew berry and I planted it in the garden of my court and it grew up there until it was as big as a man. Then I removed it from the garden and planted it on the lawn of my court even, and it grew up in the centre of that lawn so that I could fit with a hundred warriors under its foliage, and it protected me from wind and rain, and from cold and heat ...

This poem originates from the oral tradition of the bards. An extensive knowledge of places and customs was essential for one who could be called upon at short notice to recite the history of a region or its great family to support an argument or celebrate a special occasion. (It wouldn't do to be sitting by the fire in a banqueting hall when the king shouts for proof of his noble descent and be lost for words!) Many of these poems developed from localised texts, compiled in bardic schools in different parts of the country, to help students develop an encyclopaedic knowledge of their own region.

In Fintan's unique evidence, we may have a genuine scrap of ancient local knowledge identifying the origin of the Great Yew of Ross. It points an unerring finger of reality to the yew wood of Muckross near Ross Castle in Killarney, thought to be at least 5,000 years old. The only one of its kind in Ireland – and indeed one of just three left in Europe – this rare survival from early times is most definitely 'a wood of West Munster in the west', and well removed from Carlow in the Irish midlands, where the Tree of Ross was said to stand.

Once upon a time, perhaps some travelling sage did carefully wrap berries from Muckross in a scrap of linen before heading north over bogland and moor, mountain and valley, journeying for many weeks until he reached what is now Co. Carlow. And there, perhaps he unwrapped the berries and placed them in good earth, reciting spells as he did so that one might flourish. And maybe that individual odyssey survived and became woven into the fabric of legend.

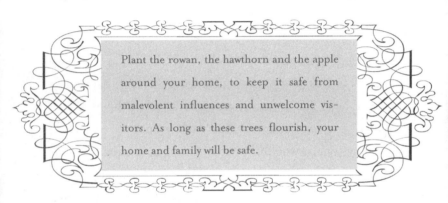

Plant the rowan, the hawthorn and the apple around your home, to keep it safe from malevolent influences and unwelcome visitors. As long as these trees flourish, your home and family will be safe.

One of the most magical trees in Irish belief was the rowan, or mountain ash. (It is still regarded as a fairy tree today.) The legend of how the rowan tree first arrived in Ireland is a lovely one, making use of many details from the legends surrounding Fionn Mac Cumhaill. On a certain occasion, it is said, the Tuatha Dé Danann agreed to play a great game of hurley against the Fianna, on the plain beside Lough Leane in Killarney. For three days and three nights they fought on the field, neither side being able to win a single goal from the other. Eventually, when the Dé Danann found that they could not overcome their rivals, they withdrew abruptly from the game and set off once more for their home underneath the hills.

The most magical tree in Irish belief is the rowan, or mountain ash.

They had, naturally enough, brought food with them on this away game: crimson nuts, arbutus apples and scarlet rowan berries, which they had carried out from the Otherworld. These fruits were strongly magical, and every care was taken that not a single apple, nut or berry should touch the earth of Ireland. However, as they passed through the Wood of Dooros, in Hy Ficra of the Moy (Co. Sligo), one of the scarlet rowan berries dropped on the earth unnoticed. From that single berry, a great rowan tree sprang up. Its berries tasted like honey, and those who ate of them felt as cheerful as if they had drunk wine or mead; and if a man who was aged 100 years ate just three berries, he would return to full health and the age of 30. Powerful fruits indeed.

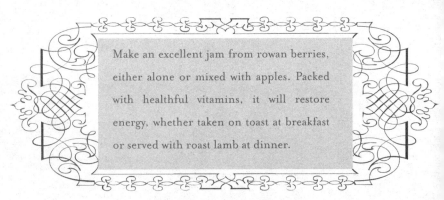

Make an excellent jam from rowan berries, either alone or mixed with apples. Packed with healthful vitamins, it will restore energy, whether taken on toast at breakfast or served with roast lamb at dinner.

Druids made a habit of sleeping on beds of rowan branches, that their dreams might be the clearer. To decide the answer to a complex problem, rowan wands inscribed with ogham symbols were thrown, the way they fell being noted and interpreted accordingly. (This is similar to the Chinese use of yarrow stalks in I Ching and indeed the casting of rune stones in other cultures.) Yew and hazel were used in the same way.

In *The Wooing of Étaín*, when the queen is spirited from her palace by the Otherworld king, Midir, the druid Dallan discovers where she is hidden by cutting four wands of yew, carving ogham symbols on them, and then casting them on the ground to see how they fall. In the *Táin*, Cúchulainn cuts ogham onto a hoop of hazel and places it on a standing stone to warn Maeve's approaching army. When discovered, the hazel hoop is put into the hands of her druids for interpretation:

> *Here is a hazel twig, what does it declare to us?*
> *What is its mystery?*
> *What number threw it,*
> *Few or many?*
> *Will it cause injury to the host,*
> *If they go a journey from it?*
> *Find out, ye druids, something therefore,*
> *For what reason it has been left here.*

When it was necessary to communicate vital messages across some distance, druids would send servants carrying wands of wood carved with ogham symbols. Few outside their circles could have translated the signs, so it was, in effect, an early method of transmitting information in code.

THE WAYS OF BIRDS AND ANIMALS

Animals and birds have been used by many cultures for augury and divination, but the killing of such creatures in order to examine their entrails for omens was never practised in Ireland.

Instead the wise ones watched and noted the movements and behaviour of wildlife, and drew their conclusions from what they saw.

Birds in particular were seen as a link between this and the Otherworld, and thought by druids to possess much knowledge about events past, present and future. The bird of choice for druidic divination was the wren. Indeed, the Irish name for the wren, *an dreoilín*, is thought to derive from *draoi ean*, or 'druid bird'. A rare scrap of ancient lore, inscribed on the margin of another document by a monk who evidently realised the value of recording the older beliefs, has preserved some of the interpretations:

> *If the little white-headed one call to thee from the east, if it be on the ground behind thee, thy wife will be taken from thee by force ... If it call from many crosses there is a slaughter of men, and the number of times it alights on the ground is the number of deaths it announces, and the quarter towards which it puts its face, from thence are the dead it announces ...*

Quite apart from suggesting that these methods were most often called upon in times of warfare and danger, this does show that the druids were conversant with the wren's characteristic habits of quick, constant movement and energetic voice; a wren will always be active and vocal. (Describing this tiny creature as 'white-headed' is a term of affection. Even today, a small child will be called *leanbhín bán óg*, or 'little fair/white-headed one'.)

The bird of choice for druidic
divination was the wren.

Druids also used ravens for determining the future, but here they
relied on the precise sounds the bird made – another practical choice,
since ravens are known for their wide range of calls and croaks.

*If the Raven croaks over a closed bed within the house, this
denotes that a distinguished guest is coming to you. But there
is a difference between them. If he be an ordinary man that
is to come, it is 'bacach! bacach!' the Raven says, but if it be
someone of importance, it is 'Gradh! Gradh!' and it is far in
the day that he croaks. If it be a soldier or a satirist that is
coming, it is 'grog, grog' or 'grob grob' that it croaks, and it
is behind you that it speaks, and it is from that direction the
guests are to come. If it be in a small voice that the Raven
speaks, 'err, err' or 'ur, ur', there is sickness to come on some
person in the house, or on some of its cattle ...*

THE TRAINING OF A DRUID

It took years to become a druid, and there were druidic schools
of learning throughout Ireland. One of the most renowned was
at Bangor in Co. Down, where later a monastic settlement was
founded over the earlier pagan site. Another, at Cruachan Ai in
Connacht, was dedicated to Manannán Mac Lir.

Emain Macha (Navan Fort) in Co. Armagh was the High King's seat and the home of the druid Cathbad.

As well as training druids, these schools also catered for the children of the nobility. The young Cúchulainn joined the other members of the youth group at Emain Macha (Navan Fort) in learning the old poems and texts from the druid Cathbad, and indeed it was Cathbad who foretold the boy's future greatness as well as the shortness of his life. A female druid called Brigit had a school in Kildare where she trained young women in the skills and knowledge of the ancient arts. Later the Christian Church would superimpose a history of their own St Brigid and her convent over the original druidic centre.

Some sources suggest that the great druidic schools of learning were held in caves and forests, but while the keepers of the ancient wisdom certainly favoured such places for ritual purposes, schooling for young pupils was a different matter. *The*

Book of Aicill suggests an extremely sophisticated educational system:

> *And Cennfaeladh was brought to the house of Briciu of Tuam Drecain at the meeting of the three streets, between the house of three ollamhs* [professors or learned men]. *And there were three schools in the town, a school of literature, a school of law and a school of poetry, and whatever he used to hear rehearsed in the three schools every day, he had by heart every night.*

This school of learning was near today's Tomregan in Co. Cavan and only a short distance from Magh Slécht, where the faithful flocked to worship or ask questions of Crom Cruaich.

Forests and caves were favoured by druids for ritual purposes.

In all such schools, the emphasis was on learning by heart. Druidic knowledge was handed down orally and committed to memory. This was partly to develop the strength and retention of the mind, but also to protect the ancient charms, spells, rites and traditions that were not to be made accessible to others by being written down. Julius Caesar, always interested in local habits and customs, observed of the druids in Gaul:

> *They do not think it proper to commit these utterances to writing, although in almost all other matters, and in their public and private accounts, they make use of Greek letters.*

It took at least 20 years to reach even the lowest levels of druidic training. Students could become poets or bards, experts in law, or augurers. Beyond that, like the shaman of other lands, to reach the highest levels of enlightenment required study and time spent alone in a remote place, usually fasting to the edge of starvation, in order to reach the elevated state of consciousness required for contact with another world. Many of the later hermits of Christian legend would, in fact, have been druids of the earlier culture, their stories made over and reshaped to fit the doctrine of Rome. An ancient *Life of St Colmcille*, preserved in the *Leabhar Breac*, reveals that his mother consulted a druid as to his education, and that the druid became Colmcille's first tutor. Did the famed saint have an earlier existence as a follower of the old ways?

Throughout their lives druids sought to expand their knowledge. Some did this by travelling to other lands and learning from

Many of the later hermits of Christian legend would, in fact, have been druids of the earlier culture.

the craft masters there. The great Munster druid Mogh Ruith is said to have completed his studies in the east, in the school of no less a master than Simon Magus. Others stayed in Ireland and submitted themselves to severe ordeals, spending long periods alone in deep forests, on tiny remote islands, or in dark caves. The mysterious Oweynagat, or Cave of the Cats, at Rathcroghan in Roscommon, was believed throughout the ages to be an entrance to the Otherworld. Guarded by the Mórrígan herself, it may well have been an initiation site for druids seeking such insight.

Oweynagat, or Cave of the Cats, at Rathcroghan in Co. Roscommon, was believed throughout the ages to be an entrance to the Otherworld.

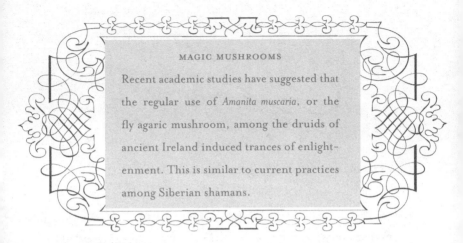

And of course there was Finegas, the venerable druid and seer who dwelt by the Boyne river and sought absolute wisdom through the Salmon of Knowledge. As it turned out, he had wisdom and awareness enough to accept that Fionn Mac Cumhaill had received it instead of himself, albeit by accident, and he was gracious in the face of Fionn's success and his own defeat.

At the heart of all druidic learning was the commitment to memory of enormous amounts of verse and poetry. A very firm distinction was drawn between these two forms. Verse, i.e. rhyme, was used for knowledge, history, the laws, since rhyming assisted in memorisation – as anyone who has had to learn poetry at school will know. And for the oldest knowledge, accuracy was essential, whether the lineage of a particular nobleman, or which individual had true right to what land. Free form poetry, on the other hand, was used to commemorate great events, such as a battle in which a great king distinguished himself, to record heroic deeds or strange happenings, and, when circumstances warranted, to pour scorn on someone in a bitter satire, or *glam dichen*.

THE *GLAM DICHEN*

The *glam dichen* was a vicious verbal attack that brought shame and disgrace and could, on occasion, inflict actual harm on the recipient. One example comes from *The Second Battle of Mag Tuiread*:

> On one occasion Coirpre, son of Etain, poet of the Tuatha Dé Danann, came to the house of Bres seeking hospitality. He entered a narrow, black, dark little house, and there was neither fire nor furniture nor bedding in it. Three small cakes were brought to him on a little dish – and they were dry. The next day he arose, and he was not thankful. As he went across the yard he said:
>
> 'Without food quickly on a dish,
> 'Without cow's milk on which a calf grows,
> 'Without a man's habitation after darkness remains,
> 'Without paying a company of storytellers – let that be
> Bres's condition.
>
> 'Bres's prosperity no longer exists,' he said. And that was true. There was only blight on him from that hour; and that is the first satire that was made in Ireland.

It is the threat of such a satire that goads Cúchulainn to fight one last time, even though he knows it will be the end of him:

> 'I will put a bad name on your kindred,' said the Druid.
> 'The news that I have been given a bad name shall never go back to that place I am never to go back to myself; for it is

little of my life that is left to me,' said Cúchulainn. And he
threw his spear ...

In another old text, it is Mongán, son of Manannán Mac Lir,
who is being threatened:

The poet said he would satirise him with his lampoons, and
he would satirise his father and his mother and his grand-
father, and he would sing spells upon their rivers, so that
fish would not be caught. He would sing upon their woods,
so that they should not give fruit, upon their plains, so that
they should be barren for ever of any produce ...

The *glam dichen* is one poetic form which has continued to
prosper throughout the ages. In playwright John B Keane's 1959
tragedy, *Sive*, he suggests that this ability has been passed down
to today's travelling people. When they are refused hospitality
by a mean-minded man, their poet immediately composes an
extempore verse:

May the snails devour his corpse,
And the rains do harm worse,
May the divil sweep the hairy crathur soon.
He's as greedy as the sow,
As the crows behind the plough,
That black man from the mountains, Seánín Rua ...

Chanted to the compelling beat of a bodhrán, the song makes the audience laugh certainly, but also makes them shiver. There is genuine venom and bad will in the words, as in all *glam dichen*. The witty 19th-century 'Curse of Doneraile' is more of a spoof than a genuine poem of ridicule, but shows its parentage clearly:

> *May Egypt's plagues at once prevail to thin the knaves of Doneraile.*
> *May frost and snow and sleet and hail benumb each joint in Doneraile.*
> *May wolves and bloodhounds trace and trail the cursed crew of Doneraile.*
> *May Oscar with his fiery flail to atoms thresh all Doneraile.*
> *May every mischief fresh and stale abide henceforth in Doneraile ...*

HEALING THE WOUNDS OF BATTLE

Druids were skilled in the arts of healing, knowing which herbs and plants to use for each affliction. In times of war, they would create a special well within the camp, bringing the most powerful plants to turn this into a magical health spa. In *The First Battle of Mag Tuiread* we are told:

> *They brought healing herbs with them, and crushed and scattered them on the surface of the water in the well, so that the precious healing waters became thick and green. Their wounded were put into the well, and immediately came out whole.*

Like the ancient Greeks, they were also hugely knowledgeable in what we might consider advanced surgical techniques. When Nuadha, king of the Tuatha Dé Danann, loses a hand in battle (and thus has to abdicate, since a king must be perfect in body), Dian Cecht crafts a new one for him, made of silver, and attaches it so skilfully that Nuadha is able to use it in a completely natural way.

This was the seventh year of Bres over Ireland, when he resigned the kingdom to Nuadha, after the cure of his hand by Dian Cecht, assisted by Creidne, the artificer, for they put a silver hand upon him.

There is a fascinating addition to the tale of Nuadha, which gives even more insight into the skills of the ancient Irish druids:

Now Nuadha was in his sickness, and Dian Cecht put on him a hand of silver with the motion of every hand therein. That seemed wrong to his son Miach. Miach went to the hand which had been replaced by Dian Cecht, and he said, 'Joint to joint of it and sinew to sinew', and he healed Nuadha in thrice three days and nights. The first 72 hours he put it against his side, and it became covered with skin. The second 72 hours he put it on his breast and Nuadha was whole.

Dian Cecht, furious that his son's skill was greater than his own, killed him. From Miach's grave grew 365 healing herbs, which were gathered in strict order as to which part of the body they appeared from, by his sister, Airmed. But Dian Cecht had the final word when he scattered the herbs so that no-one would ever again be sure which healing herb to use for which part of the body.

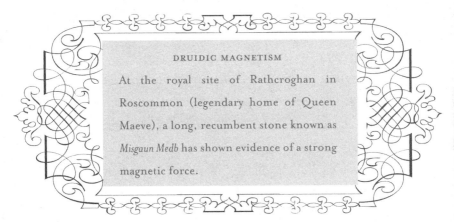

DRUIDIC MAGNETISM

At the royal site of Rathcroghan in Roscommon (legendary home of Queen Maeve), a long, recumbent stone known as *Misgaun Medb* has shown evidence of a strong magnetic force.

DRUIDIC INCANTATIONS

The wise never crossed a druid. While much of their work dealt with the peaceful arts of healing, auguring and teaching, they had other powers too. They could at will pronounce an incantation over a wisp of straw, hay or grass, which they then cast into a person's face. This would cause him or her to become a lunatic and unsettled wanderer.

One remedy for anyone thus afflicted was to find their way to the valley of Gleannagalt in Kerry, where a sacred spring was said to possess the power of curing all mental illness. Near Inishowen

The wise never crossed a druid.

Head in Donegal, the sacred well of Stroove Bran has the same virtues. All of which was helpful if the unfortunate person who offended a druid happened to live in the extreme south or the extreme north of the land, but not so good if they lived somewhere in the middle.

When it came to working magic or reciting spells, circling the sacred site three, seven or nine times while reciting the necessary charms was a key part of the ritual. This practice can still be seen in many Christian ceremonies, whether they be church novenas or feast days at a holy well.

Another powerful channelling of energy was achieved by the druid closing one eye and standing on one leg, thereby concentrating all strength in one place.

> *Lug was urging the men of Ireland to fight the battle fiercely so they should not be in bondage any longer, because it was better for them to find death while protecting their fatherland than to be in bondage and under tribute as they had been. Then Lug chanted the spell which follows, going around the men of Ireland on one foot and with one eye closed ...*

THE POWER OF THE STONES

The most advanced druids knew the secrets of the ancient stone alignments and how to channel the power contained in these, directing it for their purposes. Modern research has shown that many of these megaliths were placed with incredible accuracy on spots where several watercourses intersect underground. Such sites are known to give off electro-magnetic currents – the same ones traced by dowsers. This presumably gave additional strength to the stones, already aligned to specific phases of the sun and moon. Ceremonies held at these ritual sites under the full moon or at sunrise would have been powerful indeed. Drombeg Stone Circle near Glandore, Co. Cork, which has always been known locally as the Druid's Altar, is an example of a site where this happened.

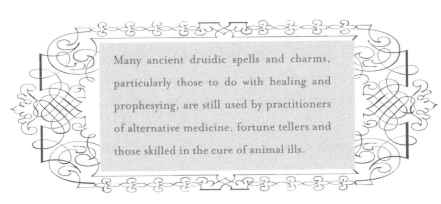

Many ancient druidic spells and charms, particularly those to do with healing and prophesying, are still used by practitioners of alternative medicine, fortune tellers and those skilled in the cure of animal ills.

The Drombeg Stone Circle, Co. Cork.

Several ancient and highly decorated ritual stones survive today, including the Turoe Stone in Galway, the Killycluggin Stone in Cavan, and the Castlestrange Stone, curiously sited halfway up the drive to a ruined mansion in Co. Roscommon. All three are granite boulders decorated with flowing spirals in the La Tène style.

Nobody knows how the Castlestrange Stone came to be in its final resting place, since there are no local legends connected with it, but it is more than likely that a covetous landowner saw it somewhere else and wasn't satisfied until he had it hauled home and placed in a highly visible position on his own driveway. The bad fortune such an action brought can be seen in the crumbling building, the rusting iron gates and the encroaching brambles further up that driveway, while the stone itself rests calm and aloof in well-trimmed surroundings. It is never a good idea to move or interfere with an ancient stone that has been set by long-ago hands in a specific place. The stories of bad luck or even death following on from such foolish behaviour are legion.

The swirling patterns of the Castlestrange Stone, Co. Roscommon, were carved more than 2,000 years ago.

Maeve of Connacht may have reigned proudly at Rathcroghan, King Conor Mac Nessa at Emain Macha, and Cormac Mac Airt at Tara, but these and other sites like Newgrange were probably used for powerful ritual purposes in even earlier times. With such history, it is understandable that later kings and queens would choose to place their palaces on such mounds of power – much in the same way that Christianity, many centuries on, would build churches on former pagan sites of worship.

THE NEED-FIRE

Ritual bonfires were very much part of the yearly cycle in ancient Ireland, kindled specifically on the great Celtic festivals of Samhain, Imbolc, Bealtaine and Lughnasa, as well as other important occasions, such as midwinter and midsummer solstices, to ensure the health and fertility of both land and people in the months ahead. In times of crisis, such as a disease attacking animals or humans, a special need-fire was kindled to banish the affliction.

These all-important fires had to be constructed ceremonially by chosen initiates with nine sacred woods, and these could then only be ignited by an oak bow and rod, all other fires in the vicinity having been extinguished beforehand (using water brought from a sacred well). Most of the woods to be used in a ritual bonfire are recorded in several sources, but, very tellingly, no source names the full nine. The list given by McNeill in *The Silver Bough* is typical:

Choose the willow of the streams,
Choose the hazel of the rocks,

Choose the alder of the marshes,
Choose the birch of the waterfalls,
Choose the rowan of the shade,
Choose the yew of resilience,
Choose the elm of the brae,
Choose the oak of the sun.

McNeill suggests that the missing link could have been holly, ash or pine. Others consider hawthorn, with its strong pagan links, to be the most likely contender. Modern sources for kindling a need-fire, particularly those from the New World, complete the nine with the grapevine or even sandalwood, but these would have been foreign to ancient Ireland.

The list being incomplete in every early source does suggest a deliberate holding back of knowledge, as is often the case with spells. Nine is, after all, one of the most powerful numbers used in magic, and we should also remember that mystic knowledge has always been jealously guarded throughout history, passed down only from master to pupil, rarely committed to written record. Only the true initiate would know the identity of the ninth and last essential ingredient for the ritual.

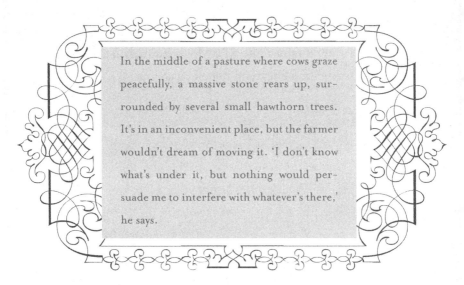

In the middle of a pasture where cows graze peacefully, a massive stone rears up, surrounded by several small hawthorn trees. It's in an inconvenient place, but the farmer wouldn't dream of moving it. 'I don't know what's under it, but nothing would persuade me to interfere with whatever's there,' he says.

TO TURN THE TIDE OF WAR

The powerful magic of druids was most needed in times of strife. A particularly descriptive passage from *The Siege of Droma Dámhgháire* gives a rare glimpse of their skills. In the heat of the battle, things are going badly for King Cormac Mac Airt of Tara against the men of Munster. He seeks the advice of his oldest druid, Ciothruadh, who immediately orders great piles of rowan wood to be cut and brought from the forest to make large fires:

> *If the smoke goes southwards, then it will be well for you to press after it on the men of Munster; and if it is hither or northward the smoke comes, then indeed it will be full time for us to retreat with all our speed.*

It isn't difficult to work out that a wind blowing towards the enemy would have the desired effect of choking and blinding them, while a strong breeze in the opposite direction would put his own men in disarray. However, the wily Mogh Ruith, Munster's chief druid, realises what is afoot and initiates a counter-spell.

He immediately ordered the men of Munster to go into the wood of Lethard and each man to bring out a faggot of the rowan tree in his hand; and that the king only should bring out a shoulder-bundle from the side of the mountain, where it had grown under three shelters, namely, shelter from the March wind, shelter from the sea wind, and shelter from the conflagration winds. The men soon returned with the wood to their camp; and the Druid Ceannmhair, Mogh Ruith's favourite pupil, built the wood up in the shape of a small triangular kitchen, with seven doors; whereas the northern fire (that prepared by Ciothruadh) on the other side was but rudely heaped up, and had but three doors. Mogh Ruith then ordered each man of the host to give him a shaving from the handle of his spear, which he mixed with butter and rolled up into a large ball, at the same time pronouncing these words in rhythmical lines:

'I mix a roaring powerful fire;
'It will clear the woods, it will blight the grass;
'An angry flame of powerful speed;
'It will rush up to the skies above,
'It will subdue the wrath of all burning wood,
'It will break a battle on the clans of Conn.'

The counter-spell works. Cormac's army flees in disarray, and the men of Munster pursue, led by Mogh Ruith in his chariot drawn by wild oxen. It calls up wonderful images, but the detail is fascinating too, revealing practical knowledge of the power of draught in building a good fire, as well as the magical qualities not just of rowan but of particular rowan, growing in a specific location and gathered by the right person.

DRUIDIC PLACENAMES

Loughnashandree, 'lake of the old druids', near Ardgroom in Co. Kerry.

Knocknadrooa, 'hill of the druids', near Skreen, Co. Sligo.

Tobernadree, 'well of the druids', near Freshford, Co. Kilkenny.

Killadroy, 'druid's wood', near Clogherny, Co. Tyrone.

Gobnadruy, 'druid's point', on Achill Island, Co. Mayo.

Derrydruel, 'druid's oak wood', near Dungloe, Co. Donegal.

The 'Druid Stone' found at Killeen Cormac, Co. Kildare, near the entrance to an Iron Age passage grave, is unique in that it is inscribed in both ogham and Latin. The ogham script reads

The old skills of healing, of fulfilling wishes, of prophesying are carried on by quiet men and women in every corner of Ireland.

'Uvan grandson of Ivacatt' while the Latin text states 'Four True Druids'. The stone now rests in the National Museum of Ireland, but its original location may have marked the honoured tomb of great power-wielding figures of the past.

Collectively the druidic elite were known as the Aos Dána, or Followers of Danu. Today Aosdána is an association of Ireland's top writers and artists, who have made major contributions to our culture.

The old skills of healing, of fulfilling wishes, of prophesying, are still carried on by quiet men and women in every corner of Ireland. They never advertise and rarely take payment, but are constantly sought out to cure an illness, suggest the right path to take, advise on love or indicate the future. There are also those who are gifted with the power to cure the ills of animals, often by no more than the laying on of hands. Like their ancient predecessors, they never reveal their knowledge and never write it down, passing it on instead to the next generation. They are the true inheritors of the ancient wisdom.

The druids of ancient Ireland were immensely wise, vastly experienced counsellors to king and commoner alike. They knew how to read the skies and the winds, how to interpret the signs given by nature and wildlife. They were also a vital link with the Otherworld, able by their advanced powers to travel and return, to ask questions and carry messages from one to the other. While much of their skill was based on a long life devoted to observation of natural phenomena and a generous endowment of commonsense, there are still enough tantalising hints to suggest at more advanced magical powers. We could all develop our powers of observation, attune ourselves better to the world around us. Whether we could, like the druids, lift the veil between this and another reality is a different question.

In Search of Powerful Women

In Ireland's earliest times, the basics of survival were the most important concerns – finding shelter, sowing crops, saving harvests, raising healthy herds, begetting children to continue the work. Ireland instinctively and naturally honoured the deities who caused the sun to shine, the rain to fall, the crops to grow.

The early deities reflected the central role of fertility, the seasons and the weather. But above all, pagan gods and goddesses symbolised the essential balance between male and female, and reflected a total reliance on nature and its powers.

The oldest 'parent' spirits of earth and sky were the Earth Mother, Danu, and the Earth Father, Crom Cruaich, but as the population grew and diversified across the land, so did the deities to whom communities turned for help. As time went on, different spirits of the Otherworld watched over different areas of every-day life, such as metalworking, fishing and farming.

But it was Danu herself who was the most revered deity of all – the goddess of fertility, the great mother who gave life to the land and her own name to the Tuatha Dé Danann.

SHEELA-NA-GIGS

These are strange (and to some, unsettling) stone carvings, mainly of women, that emphasise their sexual parts. Often found on the walls of churches or castles, they are simply a very early, down-to-earth acknowledgement of the importance of the female aspect of fertility.

The early deities reflected the central role of fertility.

Danu, the Earth Mother

anu (also known as Dana, Anu, Áine) is the all-embracing earth spirit who controls the very basis of life and the cycle of the seasons. In the oldest beliefs, not just in Ireland but across the world, any male ruler who hoped to hold his kingdom and bring prosperity to his people knew that he must, through elaborate and public ceremony, symbolically mate each year with the earth goddess, in whose hands bounteous harvests or disastrous weather lay. To neglect this ritual was to invite catastrophe.

You might well think that today, when technology appears to have supplied the answer to every problem, when scientific laboratories are the revered temples of knowledge, and smart phones, laptops and tablets have created a virtual online existence that

The Paps of Danu, near Killarney, named after the life-giving earth goddess.

can be enjoyed without ever leaving your armchair, there is little trace of this belief in the earth goddess left in Ireland. But you'd be wrong.

The old ways are still there, although not always obvious at first glance. Science, despite its vast research and unending technological experiments, still cannot control the forces of nature, and the deepest, most instinctive urge within the Irish psyche is to pay honour and homage to the oldest nature powers, the earth spirits of our land.

THE GODDESS OF FERTILITY

When life is lived close to nature, every cloudy sky, every unexpected wind change is of vital importance. All growth and nourishment comes from Danu. She cares for the land, its people, animals, crops and water sources. The personification of natural forces, in essence she *is* the land.

In old Ireland, Danu was revered in special observances at the two great dividing points of the year: the coming of summer in May and the onset of winter as October gave way to November. By gathering to praise her on these special festival days, her people could hope for good crops, healthy flocks, many children; or for a gentle winter without too much storm or cold, disease or disaster.

Today, when most of us live in comfortable, secure homes, with shopping centres and medical facilities close by, crowds still gather at the Paps of Danu, twin mountain peaks on the Cork/Kerry border, on May Day, as they have done for thousands of years. The same thing happens at Knockainey (Cnoc Áine) in Co. Limerick at the summer solstice. These and many other similar sites dedicated to the earth goddess have never been allowed to drift into oblivion. And on an everyday basis, you don't have to look too far to realise just how much Danu still plays a central role in Irish belief, although now she may be called by a different name, and given the role of mother to the figure at the very centre of Christianity.

The old ways and the old beliefs lie close under the surface of modern-day Ireland. Christianity is a highly patriarchal religion (although that is unlikely to have been its founder's original intention), but in ancient Ireland the mother goddess was all-powerful, representing as she did the vital forces of fertility, regeneration, rebirth.

If further proof be needed that the earth goddess is still deeply rooted in our culture, look no further than the many thousands of lovingly maintained grottoes with which the countryside is dotted. While displaying a plaster statue representing the mother of Christ, these are in fact, whether consciously or unconsciously, also still honouring the mother of all gods and all the land. It is no accident that children gather flowers on May Day to deck these grottoes and, in joyous song, salute the statue of Mary the Mother, as Queen of the May.

NOLLAIG NA MBAN – WOMEN'S CHRISTMAS

Take 6th January, known as the Feast of the Epiphany and also the twelfth day of Christmas. All over Ireland, women are gathering for a day of celebration or a lively evening out. No men allowed – it's strictly girls only. This is Nollaig na mBan, Women's Christmas. The modern (and rather condescending) explanation is that the exhausted housewife is allowed this one single day to herself to be free and recuperate after the efforts of the festive season. There is a lot more to the festival, though, than meets the eye.

Nollaig na mBan continues unchanged, a
memory and celebration of the unique power
of the earth goddess, and of women.

Before ever Christmas was superimposed on an older festival, pagan celebrations were always held at the midwinter solstice, hailing the turning of the year from its own death towards new birth. Though the Christian event has grown in scope and been almost swamped by commercialism, Nollaig na mBan continues unchanged, a memory and celebration of the unique power of the earth goddess, and of women.

Laillí, who grew up in the Connemara Gaeltacht in the early 20th century, remembers well how important the occasion was: 'All the women's work would be done the day before, so that there would be none left to do on the day itself.'

Then, dressed in their best aprons and shawls, they would all congregate in the chosen house for the occasion. In the meantime, the men of the house were banished, driven to walking the boreens or the fields until the women's day should be over. Girl children went with their seniors, the boys with theirs. This was one time when the division of the sexes was absolute. One woman remembered, 'It was not right for a man to be in the house on that day. It was for the women only.'

Left to themselves, the women indulged in rare treats. Tea and cake would be served, and the best reader in the group would go through *Ireland's Own* or *Old Moore's Almanac*, translating it into Irish for her listeners. After the reading came storytelling, and as dusk fell everyone made their way home. And presumably the men and boys came gratefully in out of the rain too.

Noel, an elderly man, remembers that in his youth the saying was, 'On Women's Christmas, give the men the breadknife and the tin opener and let them get on with it' – that is, that they

From Kerry to Donegal, Women's Christmas
has emerged as an exultation in the female.

would need to sort out their own food rather than being waited on by their womenfolk.

Of course, things have changed in the 21st century – but the essence remains the same. From Kerry to Donegal, Women's Christmas has emerged as an exultation in the female. Parties, shows, dinners, drinking sessions, even breakfasts are held, and they couldn't be further removed from the gentle quietness of olden Connemara. A fashionable dentist bemoans the fact that he will have to leave home while his wife throws a party, while a young waitress announces delightedly that her husband is going to have to get his own dinner, 'because I'll be off out and no two ways about it!' Every woman is out for a good time among her friends and the divil take the housework!

Theatres put on special shows to appeal to all-female audiences (male entertainers are understandably nervous about their performances on this night), and restaurants advertise special menus. The atmosphere on Nollaig na mBan is unique, totally different to the usual male/female pattern of interaction that obtains throughout the rest of the year.

'All the feminists in the world couldn't have created the bonding that happens between women at this time,' observes Eileen, a teacher who regularly holds gigantic breakfasts to which all the females of her acquaintance, from grannies to toddlers, are invited. 'It's as if it was always there, buried underneath the trappings of the Catholic Church and male domination, and exploded out when the times changed.'

In a land like ours, the old beliefs do not disappear. Centuries ago in great households, a female servant was often chosen as queen for Nollaig na mBan. In this way the family would pay honour to the goddess who might have come among them in disguise. Today, when you witness grandmothers, mothers, daughters and granddaughters, all dressed up in their best and setting out for a night of fun, deliberately banishing men from their lives for this one occasion, you are actually witnessing the continuation of one of the oldest, most atavistic rituals. They are invoking the power of ancient Ireland's matriarchal deities.

In a land like ours, the old beliefs
do not disappear.

Warmth, Wisdom & Warfare

radually, over many centuries, the central figure of the Earth goddess expanded into a tripartite role, reflecting the different aspects of her nature (a three-in-one idea later adopted most effectively by the Christian Church). In some European cultures these are identified as Maiden, Mother and Crone, but the Irish goddess chooses slightly different roles, being in one aspect caring and helpful, in another all-wise, all-knowing, and in the third, that aggressive battle queen, ready to fight at any time for her beloved land. And all three aspects – Warmth, Wisdom and Warfare – are still recognised and observed today.

WARMTH – BRIGIT: WOMAN AS HEALER

The warm, caring role definitely belongs to Brigit (also Brigid, Bríd). She is the goddess of spring, with a feast day on 1st February, or Imbolc, as it is known in the Celtic calendar. In the mild Irish climate, this is when lambs are born and ewes come back into milk. Rich, fresh milk, after a long, cold winter with limited food, is a joyful thing, and Brigit demonstrates her caring nature by this ending of hunger and the promise of full and happy months to come. Imbolc is the time to plough the fields and set the crops, prepare for the year ahead. The good health of animals, fertility, proper husbandry of lands and crops, healing, crafts, wisdom and poetry are all part of Brigit's wide brief. She is, in many ways, the familiar, approachable face of the original mother goddess and is deeply loved everywhere.

So close to and intertwined with the Irish psyche has Brigit always been that no outside influences, whether of Eastern religions or foreign colonisation, could affect her rightful place in the hearts and minds of the people. She is, in fact, the only one of the old goddesses to have survived in her name and persona right through to the present day – although many now call her a saint rather than a goddess, and pay reverence to her under the liturgical rather than the natural calendar. Her name is a constant choice for baby girls, whether Bridget, Bríd or Breda. Every county has at least one river Bride, and there are innumerable sacred wells dedicated to Brigit. Kildare town has two wells, a stone's throw from each other. The original well found itself, in modern times, on the edge of a busy road, so the local authorities, with safety in mind, created another one on a new site in a quiet laneway, not far away. After a brief period of adjustment, both came to be equally well patronised. It's the intention that counts.

There are innumerable sacred wells dedicated to both the goddess Brigit and St Brigid.

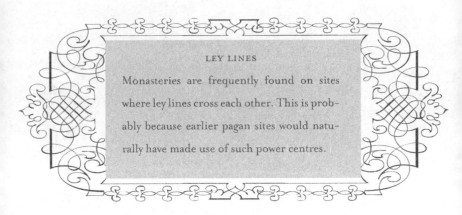

It's only fair really that Kildare should have two sacred wells since, in several legends, Brigit the goddess appears as Brigit the druid priestess, who ran a very powerful centre of healing and magic in Kildare. This may well have been a genuine druidic figure to whom supplicants came from all over the land to get advice, to seek healing, to find out what the future held, and in those tales we may have yet another example of genuine historic fact recalled in folk memory and enshrined in legend. When the Christian Church came to write a life of their St Brigid, it was no accident that they located the site of her convent on the selfsame spot in Kildare, replacing powerful druidess and virgin trainees with mother abbess and her saintly nuns.

There is, however, a key difference here: the power element. Nuns (and indeed female Christian saints) are interceders, pleaders to a powerful patriarchal god on behalf of the supplicants, whereas Brigit and her goddess sisters wield their own power.

WISDOM – THE CAILLEACH

The second aspect of the ancient Irish mother goddess is the Cailleach, or Old One, who personifies the experience of age and is the guardian of the old magic, the sacred knowledge. While Brigit rules the spring and summer, the dark winter months belong to the Cailleach, who holds the secrets of marriage, healing, childbirth, death and rebirth.

The original Cailleach has come down to us through the ages, changing and adapting over the generations, to appear as the wise woman, the witch, the seer and soothsayer, a vital person in any

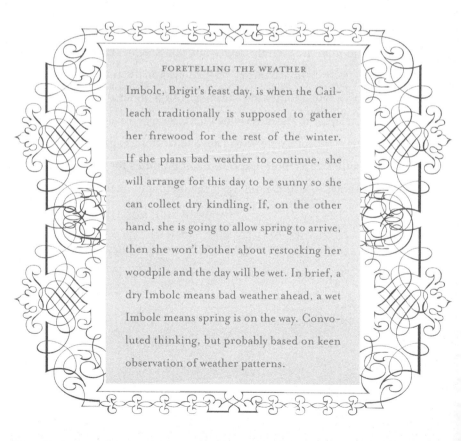

FORETELLING THE WEATHER

Imbolc, Brigit's feast day, is when the Cailleach traditionally is supposed to gather her firewood for the rest of the winter. If she plans bad weather to continue, she will arrange for this day to be sunny so she can collect dry kindling. If, on the other hand, she is going to allow spring to arrive, then she won't bother about restocking her woodpile and the day will be wet. In brief, a dry Imbolc means bad weather ahead, a wet Imbolc means spring is on the way. Convoluted thinking, but probably based on keen observation of weather patterns.

community, resorted to in times of sickness, danger or need. The word 'witch' comes from the older nature-based religion Wicca, which threatened from the outset the single-god patriarchal beliefs of later centuries. The image of a hideous old hag at her cauldron is one promoted by those male-dominated religions that sought to overthrow the female side of balanced power, and demonised these guardians of the old ways, turning them into figures to be feared, hated and persecuted, instead of venerated for their knowledge.

Despite fierce persecution throughout the ages, wise women have always been sought after for their skills with herbs and cures, their knowledge of the old ways and magical spells. Whether you wanted a young man to love you, an animal to recover, or even bad luck to attend an unfriendly neighbour, you sought out the local wise woman. In many countries this led eventually to the appalling cruelty of witch hunts and burnings, often under the name of religion. Ireland, however, does not have an extensive history of that persecution, compared with England or France, for example. It is likely there was more respect in communities for those who retained knowledge of the old ways, the old nature magic.

Wise women have always been sought after for
their skills with herbs and cures.

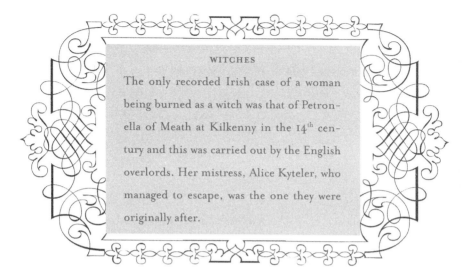

There are still wise women to be found today in both countryside and city, to be consulted for cures, spells, potions, the best time to undertake an important task, the route to recovery from an illness or sorrow. You will only be told how and where to find them, though, if you are completely trusted by the locals.

'There's still folk going to see the ones who'd know, who'd help them, but they wouldn't let on,' says one. 'Time was, you'd have the priest down on you if you were known to be consulting one of the old women!'

Joe, a country farmer, describes how one such venerable female always followed the running water, never the paved roadways. Streams and rivers have always been known to possess magical powers and indeed if you are unfortunate enough to be pursued by an ill-intentioned spirit, the sure way to escape is to cross running water. (As indeed the threatened fox will instinctively do when the hunt is in hot pursuit.)

Ireland lay at the furthest edge of the known world; no-one knew what lay beyond.

The Cailleach is also said to be wife to the sea god Manannán Mac Lir, and thus indissolubly linked with the sea, especially the western ocean. After all, for thousands of years, Ireland lay at the furthest edge of the known world, and no-one knew what lay beyond. It was out there to the west, therefore, that ancient legends grew up around the magical island of Hy Brasil, which can only (and rarely) be glimpsed at sunset, and also the fabled land of Tír na nÓg, or Land of Youth, only experienced normally by those who have left this mortal world for the immortal one. The Cailleach, goddess of death and rebirth, watches over these pathways, pointing the way to joy and freedom. She is also invoked for safety on the ocean, as is her Christian successor, Mary, with one of her most beautiful titles, 'Star of the Sea'.

Place names honouring the Cailleach abound. Ceann Caillí (Hag's Head) at the southernmost tip of the Cliffs of Moher in Clare; Sliabh na gCailleach at Loughcrew in Meath; Baile na gCailleach at Clogher Head in Co. Louth; Leabacallee, or Cailleach's Bed, in Glanworth, Co. Cork. But to discover evidence that reverence for the Cailleach is still alive and vibrant to this day, go to the remote Kilcatherine peninsula in West Cork.

The Hag of Beara, Co. Cork, is seen as a powerful symbol of the mother goddess.

Here, at the top of a hill overlooking Cailleach Bay, stands the legendary great grey rock An Cailleach Beara, or the Hag of Beara. Said to have lived more than seven lifetimes before turning to eternal stone, the Hag is one of the strongest manifestations of the mother goddess. It is the subject of a 10th-century Irish poem, 'The Lament of the Old Woman of Beare', which mourns the passing of a golden, heroic, pre-Christian age.

Come to this silent monument at any time of the day, any time of the year, and you will find tracks through the heather, tiny worn pathways leading towards the rock. All over its surface, in crevices, hollows, wherever there is sufficient space, coins, pebbles, trinkets and other small offerings are placed. Visitors to the Cailleach Beara may have discovered it on the internet from thousands of miles away and found their way along the twisting roads of the Beara Peninsula by GPS, may have taken pictures with their mobile phones to transmit instantly to friends across the world; but there on that remote headland, looking out over the western seas, they instinctively revert to the old ways and pay homage to the goddess who holds the secrets of life and death.

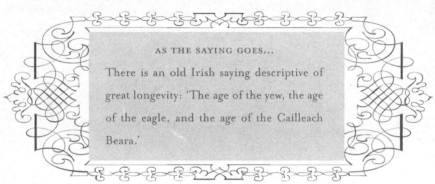

AS THE SAYING GOES...

There is an old Irish saying descriptive of great longevity: 'The age of the yew, the age of the eagle, and the age of the Cailleach Beara.'

WARFARE – THE MÓRRÍGAN

In her warlike aspect, the great goddess was the feared Mórrígan (Great or Phantom Queen), fierce, wild, demanding, implacable. She it was who oversaw and manipulated every famous battle of ancient Ireland, championing one side or the other as she perceived the rights and wrongs of the dispute, or indeed as the humour took her. As we will see, the notorious Queen Maeve of Connacht was a semi-historical daughter of the Phantom Queen.

Also known as Badb or Macha, the Mórrígan often appears as a raven flying over the thick of the bloodshed, or driving her war chariot through the battle lines. As one of the Tuatha Dé Danann, she used her powers to fight invaders: the Fir Bolg at the First Battle of Mag Tuireadh, for example, and the Fomorians at the Second. As a goddess she could – and often did – use magic to take the side of one chieftain or petty king against another – always assuming that her protégé would recognise her power and give her due reverence.

The tales of the Mórrígan appearing as a hideous old hag who demands that the hero pledge her his love echo the old idea of a great king symbolically mating with a goddess to maintain power. (Later fairy tales, such as *Beauty and the Beast* or *The Frog Prince*, would switch the male and female roles in these stories. By that time, it was acceptable to have a hideous male challenging an innocent girl, but the converse was not.) If the hero has the courage to accept the hag's advances, she transforms into a beautiful woman who leads him to victory. If he retreats in disgust, his chances of survival are slim.

Cúchulainn refused the Mórrígan and she, in the shape of a raven, perched on his shoulder at the moment of his death, cawing in triumph. Such details as these in ancient legend generally represent the war between goddess-based pagan ways and the newer rituals of Christianity that put men, not women, in the leading role.

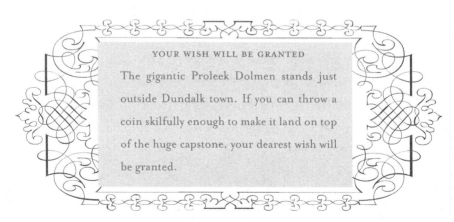

YOUR WISH WILL BE GRANTED

The gigantic Proleek Dolmen stands just outside Dundalk town. If you can throw a coin skilfully enough to make it land on top of the huge capstone, your dearest wish will be granted.

Maeve, the Warrior Queen

he mountain of Knocknarea rises proudly from the surrounding plains on Sligo's Cuil Irra peninsula. In Irish it's called Cnoc na Rí, the Royal Hill. You don't have to wonder why for long – Queen Maeve's Tomb, on the very pinnacle, is clearly visible from miles away. It's an ancient ritual site but, despite its historic status, it has never been excavated. Legend has it that to do so would be to awaken the wrath of a goddess queen whose anger is not easily appeased. And it would not be a good idea to annoy Maeve. Never was. Touchy would be understating it. And so, her peace undisturbed, Queen Maeve lies sleeping on Knocknarea, awaiting the day when Ireland has need of her once more.

Queen Maeve lies sleeping on Knocknarea, which translates as 'Royal Hill' in Irish.

BREHON LAW AND FEMALE POWER

Irish women throughout the ages have always been individualistic, determined, powerful. Fond of getting their own way, some might say. Fully aware of their importance, would be more like it. More than 1,000 years ago, before Norman-English rule, this status was reflected in the law; women had more rights and freedoms than most other countries then – and even some now. Our ancient Brehon laws enshrined certain women's rights, such as the continued ownership of their property after marriage, that the female half of the world is still struggling to re-establish in the 21st century.

Alas, those original Irish laws are now history. Male-dominated religious, political and legal systems did their utmost to eliminate this abhorrent female power and stamp out the notion of women having equal status, substituting instead a culture where masculine rule was absolute and women were subservient, second-class creatures. Although successful in many ways, particularly in the establishment of a decisively male-oriented legal system, that instinctive inheritance of the Irish woman could never quite be eradicated. The warrior queen survives, deep in the unconscious, and you will see the same strength and individuality, the same determination, in a red-haired woman striding along a country road today as you would have seen when Queen Maeve drove her chariot to battle at the head of her vast army.

The warrior queen survives, deep in the Irish unconscious.

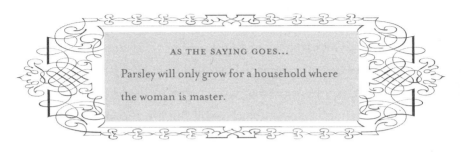

THE STORY OF THE *TÁIN*

The legendary Maeve, half-historic human ruler of Connacht
and half-*sidhe* (fairy), looks both forward and backward. She is,
in fact, a direct descendant of the oldest earth goddesses to whom
Ireland first gave reverence. So, indeed, are all those gentle, seduc-
tive women with siren songs and golden hair, who appear clad in
wondrous, glittering robes in romantic legends, riding magnificent white horses, seducing young heroes away to Tír na nÓg.

Maeve, though, is definitely battle queen rather than seduc-
tress. What she wants, she takes by force. That is how the *Táin
Bó Cúailnge* (*The Cattle Raid of Cooley*) presents it anyway. Our
greatest surviving epic tale, transmitted orally for centuries before
finally being written down around the late 11th century, it paints
a vivid picture of the Celtic chivalric code, where kingdoms wage
war as much for honour as for gain, and a mighty queen chooses
for herself what (or indeed whom) she desires. It's refreshingly
different to the English romantic legends of later centuries where
sad and soulful maidens wait hopefully in remote castles for a
prince to come by. Waiting to be rescued is not part of the Celtic
woman's heritage. Go-getting is where it's at, whether by war or
by seduction. Or both, if necessary.

Most of the *Táin* is concerned with the pitched battles between the men of Connacht, led by Maeve and her husband Ailill, and the men of Ulster, championed by Cúchulainn. But it is the surprisingly funny prologue that gives a glimpse of the real power and independence that a woman could enjoy in ancient Ireland.

Lying comfortably in bed with his wife one night, Ailill is unwise enough to suggest to Queen Maeve that she was fortunate when she married him. Her sharp query as to why this might be should warn him, but it doesn't. Happily oblivious to the chill creeping into the abode of connubial bliss, deaf to the rumbles of approaching thunder, he goes on smugly to enumerate just how much wealth he has brought to the partnership. Instantly she snaps back that she has brought more. He disagrees. She starts listing:

> *I gave you a contract and a bride-price as befits a woman, namely, the raiment of 12 men, a chariot worth thrice seven cumals, the width of your face in red gold, the weight of your left arm in white bronze. Whoever brings shame and annoyance and confusion on you, you have no claim for compensation of honour-price for it, except what claim I have, for you are a man dependent on a woman's marriage-portion.*

Ailill caps Maeve's list. Furious, Maeve flings back the rich coverlets and storms out to the great hall, calling for servants to bring all their separate wealth immediately, this minute, without delay, and lay it out so the argument can be settled.

Sleepy servants rub their eyes and yawn as they stumble from treasure chest to store cupboard, dropping gold cups, tripping over silver chains, and wondering why on earth their lord and lady have chosen this hour of the night to do a stock control check.

Despite her confident claims, when it comes down to the very last detail Maeve discovers that she has nothing to match a magnificent white bull owned by Ailill. Worse, that bull had originally been born into one of her own herds, but had, apparently, disdained being owned by a woman and had taken himself off to her husband's fields, according to the story. (Interesting that the bull's right to change ownership like this is not disputed at all.)

This point, from which all the battle slaughter of the *Táin* develops, is a reflection of the importance of cattle in ancient Ireland. Ultimately, how much you were worth was reckoned in cows, not coinage. For Maeve, this is disaster, and she descends into total despair. To be less than her husband is unthinkable. Lacking that one single bull, her life is not worth living.

Despair doesn't last long. It generally doesn't with warrior queens. They don't get to the top by being weaklings, accepting defeat. Maeve sends out search parties. And soon they're back, hastened as much by her threats as the promise of reward. Yes,

Ultimately, how much you were worth was reckoned in cows, not coinage.

OLD WAYS, OLD SECRETS

there is another such paragon. The Brown Bull of Cooley. But he belongs to Ulster, the sworn enemy of Connacht.

There are more twists ahead in the plot. Not a whit deterred by a little matter like sworn enmity, Maeve sends fleet-footed messengers to Daire, the bull's owner, asking no more than to borrow his fine beast for a year (by which time the bull would, presumably, have more than made up any gaps in her own herds). As part of the bargain, she quite matter-of-factly offers herself to Daire for a night of magnificent pleasure. A queen might choose her partners as whim, diplomacy or amusement suggested. Shy and modest, these leading ladies of ancient Ireland were not. Cleopatra would have recognised a kindred sister. Ailill's thoughts on the matter are not recorded; he is but the son of a king, whereas his wife is absolute queen in her own right.

Not surprisingly, Daire is delighted to agree to Maeve's offer and throws a lavish banquet for her messengers to celebrate the happy outcome. Unfortunately, he chances to hear Maeve's servants boasting over their wine cups that they would have taken the bull anyway, agreement or no, and carried it back triumphantly to Connacht. Furious, he cancels the agreement and sends them off with a flea in their ear instead of a bull on a leash. Which leaves Maeve with no option but to declare war.

And so the *Táin* unfolds. Armies become locked in mortal combat, friend fights friend, Cúchulainn emerges as a hero, Maeve consults the fates and uses witchcraft, and there is general mayhem and slaughter across the land. In the end the two bulls fight each other to the death. Everybody loses, in fact, which is often the way with war.

The *Táin* is a fine example of legend and history blending into one magnificent epic. It is likely that the kingdoms of Connacht and Ulster (as indeed Munster and Leinster, Leinster and Connacht, and every other permutation) fought each other many times, and that powerful figures, whether of legend or history, became incorporated into these events. While the text is superbly embroidered and embellished, with many a sidetrack and frequent distractions, it almost certainly contains folk memory of genuine events in the Ireland of long ago.

From another viewpoint, however, Maeve challenging the young Cúchulainn, who holds the Gap of the North against the invading army, could well echo once again the confrontation between the older, goddess-based beliefs, and the newer, warrior-based structure that was to succeed with the coming of the Celts.

The battle slaughter of the *Táin* reflects the importance of cattle in ancient Ireland.

The Banshee

As we have seen, in ancient times it was the Mórrígan who had a menacing role as harbinger of Fate to noble families, whether appearing to great warriors before major battles, or turning up in the midst of a banquet to bring bad tidings. And it is this Fate aspect of the goddess that has survived to the present day – as the famous and dreaded Banshee.

The Banshee (*bean sidhe*, or fairy woman) is a strange enigma in modern Ireland. Every man, woman and child knows of her, and you don't have to go very far to find real-life experiences. Renowned for foretelling imminent death, she sends her long-drawn-out and eerie wail across wild and empty landscapes. She is also known to proclaim her presence in urban environments by three sharp knocks on the front door – be warned that you must at all costs resist the overwhelming urge to answer this peremptory summons. She's been around as long as our folklore has been recorded, and in all likelihood a long time before that; appearing in every generation right through to the modern day. Most often heard, rarely seen, she is known by the alternative title of the Baobh (pronounced 'bough' or 'buff') in some parts of the country.

The unique fact about the Banshee is that, throughout the ages, unlike other spirit figures, she has resisted change, remaining today exactly as she has always been, a true relic of our pagan past. When you look closely at other Irish customs and beliefs, it is easy to trace the gradual alteration over time, under the pressure of established religion. The goddess Brigit, for example, is changed from powerful, independent figure to a saint on the sidelines, while supreme goddess Danu can barely be distinguished today underneath the countrywide profusion of grottoes containing statues of a meek Virgin Mary. Sacred springs and wells where once the water spirits were worshipped are now designated firmly under the guardianship of one Christian saint or another.

Yet somehow the Banshee has escaped the chains and the enslavement, the determined makeover and the downward spiral. From ancient times, when she was a feared aspect of the Mórrígan, she holds still her power and her identity. She alone remains unalterably of the Otherworld, continuing to call to our deepest, most atavistic instincts. And that makes her an enigma indeed.

Renowned for foretelling imminent death, she sends her long-drawn-out and eerie wail across wild and empty landscapes.

THE CURSE: WHO HEARS THE BANSHEE?

Some say that this supernatural death messenger will appear only to five old Irish families: the O'Briens, O'Neills, O'Gradys, O'Connors, and Kavanaghs. Others insist that she follows any Irish family (especially those with Mac or O in their name). But the Banshee is heard anywhere and everywhere, by all kinds of people, even visitors to this country who may never have heard of her before.

She strikes absolute terror into the hearts of those who hear the eerie wailing or the fateful three knocks at the door. Comfortingly, she is never heard by those whose time has actually come, but by others – sometimes relatives and friends, but quite often by complete strangers who happen to be nearby. Her lament has also been heard at the original family home of an exile who is about to pass on. Though humans may travel, it seems that the Banshee prefers to remain on Irish soil.

THE DEATH COACH

In some parts of Ireland, instead of the Banshee, the Death Coach (often also called the *Cóiste Bodhar,* or Silent Coach), driven by a headless coachman, comes to collect the departing soul. If you hear it approaching, the only thing to do is ensure all gates are thrown wide open. It may then pass by without stopping. But woe betide those who forget and leave a gate closed …

The Banshee legend, born of lonely countryside and dark nights, refuses to vanish in the face of fluorescent street lighting and neat housing estates.

There are those, of course, who will claim that the Banshee, like so many other figures of legend, belongs to the 'good old days' before electricity banished the shadows from farmhouse kitchens, when whole communities, with no distractions of television or electronic games, clustered by the fireside to hear *shanachies* retell the much-loved stories. Innocent times, they declare smugly. Today we know better. But do we?

You have only to ask around, and before long it becomes clear that the Banshee is still very much with us. Not just in the countryside but in our towns and cities too. Despite modern technology, space-age travel, super-speed world communications, and more information than we could ever need at the click of a button, the enigma that is the Banshee remains very much part of Ireland and the Irish psyche.

Ask anywhere, be it pub, café, shop or college. At first you will get the obligatory embarrassed laugh, then a wary glance. Eventually, as soon as they are persuaded that the query is genuine and not born of a desire to poke fun, the experiences start to flow.

'My father always claimed he heard her one night, when he was coming home,' admits Denis, a supermarket manager. 'He said it made his hair stand on end.'

'Oh yes, we have the Banshee in our family,' said Cliona, a young nurse, quite matter-of-factly. 'It's because we're MacSweeneys. It's about two years now, though, since we last heard the knock ...'

THE DULLAHAN

The driver of the Death Coach is some-times the Dullahan, but this spectral figure is more usually seen riding a black horse across the hills, his head tucked firmly under his arm with eyes darting from side to side and mouth stretched in a hideously wide grin. If he stops and calls out a name in a ringing voice, that person is marked for death. The Dullahan tends to keep to the northern half of Ireland, while the Banshee holds the south.

The Dullahan, a foreteller of death, rides a black horse across the hills of the north of Ireland.

Sightings of the Banshee are more unusual. Bríd told me that her father-in-law, who was in the army at the time, was driving an army truck back from manoeuvres in the early hours of the morning. As they came to the outskirts of the town, he saw something strange fluttering in front of an upstairs window in a tall house. At first, he thought it was a sheet left out by accident – and it was only as they drew nearer he realised that it was the shape of a wraith-like woman with flowing robes and long hair. The lorry windows were shut, so he didn't hear her cries, but he drove frantically on to the barracks, where his men, who hadn't seen anything, had to help him down, he was so shaken. The next morning he discovered that a woman had died in that house in the early hours of the morning. 'He never forgot that incident for the rest of his life,' said Bríd.

It is often claimed by those who have not experienced the Banshee that the eerie sound must simply have been a vixen yowling or a barn owl screeching. Whatever other solutions may be offered to the mystery, this presumption is as exasperating and ill-founded as it is patronising. Are they really claiming that those who live in the countryside, close to nature in all its forms, would not recognise the bark of a fox or the cry of an owl? Indeed, in the body of evidence collected by a 1970s survey into Banshee sightings, it was notable that many of the hearers themselves actually compared the cry with that of familiar animals. Said one country dweller: 'It would put you in mind of a vixen and she screeching, but a vixen will stop and listen for the dog fox every now and then. This went on and on and on, the way no animal could do.'

I put the question to John-Joe, an elderly farmer who claims to have heard the Banshee several times, that he might have mistaken the call of a fox. His face darkens and he thumps the table. 'Woman, do you not understand? It's like nothing else on earth, and if you're meant to hear it, then hear it you will!'

His wife comes in with a tray of tea and he gestures towards her. 'She has it in her family too, but it's the knock they hear.'

Startled, I glance up and the woman nods matter-of-factly. 'It was my uncle the last time I heard it. Oh, it scares the life out of you!'

Breda, a no-nonsense local councillor, first heard it when she was a child. 'It was late, a dark winter's night, and I was in the back kitchen on my own when I heard this dreadful screaming outside. It was like nothing I'd ever heard in my life before and it totally freaked me out. I ran into the front room and asked my mother if she'd heard it, and she said, "That's the banshee." I've never forgotten it.'

On the next occasion, when she was a teenager, Breda actually saw it – as did several others. 'I was in the youth club and this night a bunch of us were coming home. It was just when we were passing a big rock that we saw this white figure just floating across in front of the car. I could see it was a woman, in white draperies,

'It's like nothing else on earth, and if you're meant to hear it, then hear it you will!'

with some sort of veil over her head. I got the idea that she was young and kind of elegant, but we only saw it for a moment and it was gone. Myself and two of the lads said, "What in Heaven's name was that?" and the priest, who must have been as shaken as we were, said, "I think we'll just say a decade of the Rosary."'

Why *is* the Banshee as powerful an image in modern Ireland as she was in ancient times, still accepted almost as part of everyday life? Pervasive, perpetually renewing itself, the Banshee's legend, born of wild, lonely countryside and dark nights, refuses to vanish in the face of fluorescent street lighting and neat housing estates. Perhaps more than any other spirit of Ireland's ancient beliefs, the Banshee is still very much with us today.

THE COMB

In some parts of the country, the Banshee is said to comb her long hair as she laments. Should you find a black comb by the roadside, do not touch it on any account. There are many folktales of men daring to carry such an object home, only to have the Banshee battering in fury at their windows that night. In such cases, it is advisable to hold the comb in a pair of fire tongs when returning it to its rightful owner.

Beyond the Mist: Gods of Old

The supernatural females of Celtic Ireland had, of course, many powerful male counterparts, including the oldest of them all, Crom Cruaich.

Among the Tuatha Dé Danann, one of the best-loved pagan gods was the Dagda, or Good God, who was a happy, fatherlike figure. In addition to possessing the cauldron of plenty, he had a magical harp that could change feelings or even seasons with its wonderful music. It was famed for three legendary pieces: the tune of sorrow, the tune of battle, and the tune of happiness. It is said that these special tunes survive even today inside the fairy forts of the Good People, and sometimes a traveller falling asleep unknowingly against the wall of such a place will hear music such as he has never heard before. When he wakes next morning, though, he will be unable to remember how it went – only that it was supremely beautiful.

Lugh was the god of sun and light who, besides being all-powerful in battle, also looked after the crops, and is thus the worthy successor of Crom Cruaich, the older earth god. His main feast was the great harvest festival that is still commemorated at the beginning of the month which bears his name, Lughnasa, or, as the Romans later christened it, August.

Dian Cecht was the god of healing, who saved the Tuatha Dé Danann from defeat in battle many a time with his skills.

Goibniu was the god of metalwork, his importance reflecting the reverence in which metalworking was held. Without that skill, ploughshares could not turn the land to sow seed, warriors could not bear their swords and spears into battle, kings and queens would have no exquisitely worked gold collars and bracelets to show off their status.

Manannán Mac Lir was the god of the sea and seafaring, of boats and fishing, creator of storms and saviour of sailors. On a small island like Ireland, where the unpredictable sea is an inescapable part of everyday life, he needed placating in times of storm and danger. He was husband to the Cailleach Beara, she who held life and death in her hand. However, he had other wives among the Tuatha Dé Danann, notably the beautiful Fand.

But the best-known and most important of the gods of ancient Ireland was Crom Cruaich (or Crom Dubh), the crooked or dark god, who was the all-powerful earth father.

Crom Cruaich, the Earth Father

On Boa Island in Lower Lough Erne there stands a mysterious little statue of ancient origin. Unusually, the statue has a face on either side, one sternly masculine, the other smiling and almost feminine. Below each face are the vestiges of what seem to be crossed arms. Where it came from, what it is doing in a tiny churchyard, no-one can say. But to one side, lying on the grass, is a broken pillar that clearly was once part of the statue. Look closely. Yes, there are the carved hands, completing the crossed arms. But if that heavy piece were somehow put back in place – and you can't help longing to do it – the arms of each would then come round at the sides and the hands would link one side of the statue with the other. Could this be an example of the male and female earth deities, a recognition in stone that both are essential to balance life?

WHO IS CROM CRUAICH?

The Boa Island statue has a face on either side, one masculine, the other almost feminine.

In earlier times, Ireland had its primary male god to counterbalance the earth goddess, Danu. Known usually as Crom Cruaich, the crooked god, he has a more fearful and threatening aspect than the all-loving mother of the land. You might run to the earth mother for comfort, but you tiptoed into the earth father's domain to beg for favours. Legends, traditions, scraps of ancient texts speak of the need to appease, to offer sacrifice, to tremble before this powerful presence that could wreak havoc as easily as dispense good fortune. A god of fertility, certainly, but also master of the storm, the lightning bolt, the flood and the famine – and, some say, of bloody sacrifice.

The Annals of the Four Masters, compiled by monks from old texts and folk memory, recorded that a great centre of worship for Crom Cruaich did once exist:

This was the principal idol of all the colonies that settled in Ireland, from the earliest period to the time of St Patrick, and they were wont to offer to it the firstlings of animals, and other offerings.

The site, known as Magh Slécht, or the Plain of Prostrations, was located in what is now rural Cavan, close to the Monaghan border, in the barony of Tullyhaw. Today this is a peaceful and empty landscape, but in early Ireland, it was an important place of worship, drawing numbers of supplicants each year seeking blessings, good harvests, and answers to their prayers. An old reference in ogham writing reads: 'In it, Cruaich was and twelve idols of stone around him and himself of gold.'

Here, facing Lough Garadice, rose a sacred hill, on the summit of which stood a banked enclosure, or *rath*. Entering, the faithful would face the frightening stone image of Crom Cruaich. A bent and crooked monolith, Crom was circled by 12 lesser standing stones – courtiers who emphasised his strength and power. No wonder the visitors prostrated themselves.

Is it coincidence that Boa Island and its strange two-faced statue lie only a few miles from Magh Slécht? That statue may be the only record we have of Ireland's ancient acknowledgement that balance in the life force is necessary, female and male, goddess and god, yin and yang.

Crom means 'leaning' or 'bent', while Cruaich in Old Irish means 'rick', i.e. of straw or hay, confirming that one of Crom's incarnations was as the harvest god. As Danu ensured the new growth of spring and summer, so Crom ensured a successful harvest and the laying up of supplies against the dark months. In some parts of the country he is still known as Crom Dubh, reflecting his darker side. This sun god could be generous, but he could also withhold his life-giving rays when he chose, bringing darkness or storm.

MAGH SLÉCHT AND ST PATRICK

When you stand in the silence of this quiet landscape, it's hard to imagine the noise of fervent worshippers all around you, tramping the grass into mud, bargaining for boat crossings, raising their eyes hopefully, perhaps fearfully, to the hill rising beyond, but this was one of the major sites of worship in the country. Significantly, it gets serious attention in the *Tripartite Life of St Patrick*, a collection of documents in Middle Irish, which claims that the doughty saint singled Magh Slécht out for special attention.

Determined to demonstrate the superior power of the new Christian religion over older customs, Patrick is said to have smitten Crom with his crozier, breaking the great monument into several pieces; he followed this up by striking each of the twelve surrounding stones so that they immediately sank deep into the earth, leaving only their heads showing. (Why didn't he simply 'rebrand' the stones as Christ and his Twelve Apostles, since the numbers and layout were so convenient? There is no record of standing stones ever being thus converted. Clearly the influence of Crom and his entourage was so great that, like Carthage, they had to be destroyed.)

Patrick then rechristened many sacred wells and established a number of churches in a rough circle around Magh Slécht, creating a Christian barricade to prevent the old religion from breaking out. He was right to be concerned about this, since within an area of barely three square miles, more than 80 prehistoric monuments have been identified, and hundreds more await discovery – yet the surrounding countryside outside that area is almost bare of similar relics. That is exceptional, even in Ireland, and testifies to the site's importance as an early place of worship.

A cryptic reference in the *Dindshenchas* (an early text on the lore of places and place names) speaks of 'the high idol with many small groups around', which may reflect the proliferation of minor supporting sites, established to do Crom Cruaich even greater honour. To bring sacred wells within the Christian ambit, to draw attention away from pagan monuments by establishing churches, was a sensible move for the new religion. One of Patrick's churches was actually built within the banks of an old *rath* or fairy fort. Today known as Kilnavert, the original name of the church was, tellingly, Fossa Slécht or Rath Slécht (the boundary or fort of Slécht).

The story of Patrick vanquishing Crom Cruaich is a good one, but it isn't supported by evidence. Earlier biographies of the saint, written not long after his death, make no mention of this event, and it only appears for the first time in the *Tripartite Life*, published some 500 years later. When the old habits of the people proved obdurate to change, the early Christian missioners could do one of two things: they could take over the gods and their

One of Patrick's churches was actually built within the banks of an old *rath,* or fairy fort.

rites, recreating them anew as saints and religious observances; or they could demonise them and compose a suitable episode in the life of a major saint showing how the old gods were overthrown by the power of Christianity.

MAGH SLÉCHT AND KING TIGHEARNMAS

Legend has it that it was an early High King, Tighearnmas, who introduced the smelting of gold here. (There is still gold to be found in our mountains, although thankfully not in large enough quantities to justify major mining projects.) The *Dindshenchas* hints that he met a dramatic end – and this may be an amalgamation of historical fact with a Christian gloss:

> *And it was at Magh Slécht that King Tighearnmas himself died, and three quarters of the men of Ireland with him, on the eve of Samhain while they were in the act of worshipping Crom Cruaich, the chief idol of Ireland.*

Did an ancient king and his men die in a particularly virulent outbreak of disease, now known as the Seventh Plague of Ireland? Were they attacked? Certainly the monk who copied the legends ascribed the catastrophe to heavenly intervention. That brief note embedded in a medieval manuscript is all we are ever likely to know of a tragedy long ago.

BELIEF AND SACRIFICE

Some ancient (and modern) scribes link Crom Cruaich with human sacrifice – and child sacrifice at that. Followers of Crom, it was claimed, were required to offer up their firstborn child to guarantee good crops. It's a suggestion that was passed on, not only by zealous Christians throughout the century, but also today by some enthusiastic websites that claim Magh Slécht is the creepiest or most haunted place on earth. It isn't. Go there and feel the calm power for yourself.

It may also have been the site of a powerful oracle, which gave answers to those who came and paid homage to Crom. Interesting to note that the old name for Lough Garadice, which faces the site, is Guth Ard, or Loud Voice. A brief reference in the 9th-century *Quarta Vita* (another version of the life of St Patrick)

Ritual sites often contain the remains of barrows, wells and standing stones, such as Killycluggin in Co. Cavan.

seems to confirm this, decrying Crom as a 'very bad demon' but admitting that he did respond to worshippers, 'wherefore they worshipped him as a god'. There is much we don't know about this Delphic echo in the heart of Ireland. What kind of person gave the oracular utterances? Did they rely on wisdom or on herbal inspiration? (Hallucinogenic herbal compounds were well known to the druids.) What kind of questions were asked?

Magh Slécht holds its secrets well. It is not even possible to pinpoint exactly the hill on which Crom Cruaich stood. One suggested site is Killycluggin, where a superbly carved single granite boulder was found. (The actual Killycluggin Stone is now in the Cavan County Museum at Ballyjamesduff, but an excellent replica stands by the roadside, marking the centrepoint of a region that once drew worshippers from far and wide.) There is also a small stone circle here, and within a radius of three miles, there are standing stones, stone rows, dolmens, barrows and wells in profusion, all found close to lakes. Or the hill might have been at the site of Kilnavert Church. What is certain is that the whole area was regarded with reverence, as evidenced by the proliferation of ancient monuments, built with the labour of many hands.

CROM'S MODERN FESTIVALS

Crom is still acknowledged in country areas as the presiding spirit of the harvest. Harvest festivals are held on the last Sunday in July or the first Sunday in August throughout the country. At Lough Gur in Co. Limerick (where the day is known as Black Stoop Sunday, reflecting Crom's gait as he carries the first sheaf of ripe corn up from the Underworld), there is a stone circle, with one great stone dwarfing all the others and known as Rannach Crom Dubh, or 'the staff of Black Crom', where offerings are left at harvest time; and at nearby Cromwell Hill is the standing stone of Caisleán Crom.

At Mount Callan, Co. Clare, in the 19th century, it was the custom to bring garlands of flowers to a specific mound known as Altoir na Greine, or the Altar of the Sun, in a ceremony known as the Gathering of Crom Dubh. In the 1870s, the local clergy put an end to such pagan practices, and forbade the people to assemble there. But now you can go there at the right time of year and find that the tradition has not been broken. It is well observed in Kerry too, where the little village of Cloghane is the centre of festivities on the last Sunday in July, Domnach Crom Dubh.

Harvest festivals are still held on the last Sunday in July or the first Sunday in August.

Heroic Warriors

〜❧〜

he heroic warrior, half god, half man, unstoppable, undefeatable, possessing amazing powers, is to be found everywhere in the legends and sagas that have been handed down. They often reflect the conflict between – or perhaps the blending of – the older Tuatha Dé Danann legends and the newer Celtic tales. A god falls in love with a mortal princess, or an Otherworld maiden comes in disguise to a human hero. Sometimes it happens unknowingly through eating an enchanted apple, or swallowing a fly in a mysterious goblet of wine. But in every case, a child is born by magical means, and that child is destined for great deeds.

Two figures stand out above all others: Cúchulainn and Fionn Mac Cumhaill.

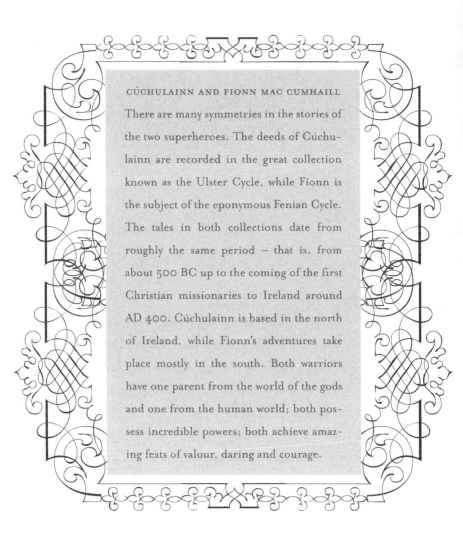

CÚCHULAINN AND FIONN MAC CUMHAILL

There are many symmetries in the stories of the two superheroes. The deeds of Cúchulainn are recorded in the great collection known as the Ulster Cycle, while Fionn is the subject of the eponymous Fenian Cycle. The tales in both collections date from roughly the same period – that is, from about 500 BC up to the coming of the first Christian missionaries to Ireland around AD 400. Cúchulainn is based in the north of Ireland, while Fionn's adventures take place mostly in the south. Both warriors have one parent from the world of the gods and one from the human world; both possess incredible powers; both achieve amazing feats of valour, daring and courage.

Cúchulainn

Cúchulainn is the son of Deichtne, sister to the Celtic High King Conor Mac Nessa of Ulster. On the morning Deichtne is to marry the nobleman chosen for her, Sualtain mac Róich, Lugh, the sun god of the Tuatha Dé Danann, catches sight of her and carries her off. When she is found by the search party, she is already with child; the baby she bears is named Setanta.

As is the way with heroic warriors, Setanta shows his extraordinary abilities from an early age, setting off for Emain Macha, the seat of the High King, when not quite seven years old. There he challenges the elite boy troops of the king and beats them all, both in the game of hurling and in hand-to-hand fighting. Whereupon, naturally, the king recognises him as his nephew and he is allowed to join the youth brigade.

HOW SETANTA BECAME CÚCHULAINN

The tale of Cúchulainn is familiar to every Irish child. King Conor Mac Nessa is invited to a great feast at the fort of his good friend, Culainn, the smith, and asks his promising young nephew to come along too. The lad, however, is in the midst of an exciting hurling match and says he will follow later. Once at the fort, with feasting well under way, the king forgets that his nephew is still to come and raises no objection when Culainn states his intention of closing the gates and loosing his fearsome guard dog. Of course, when Setanta comes along, striking his ball happily in front of him with his hurley, the hound raises his threatening voice so that everyone in the great hall hears him.

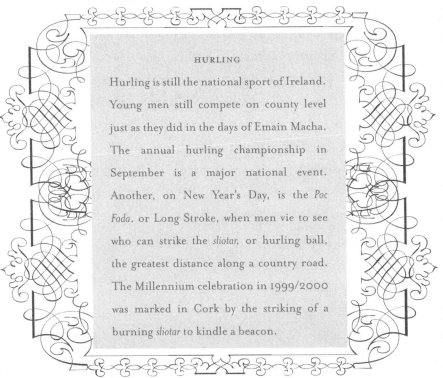

HURLING

Hurling is still the national sport of Ireland. Young men still compete on county level just as they did in the days of Emain Macha. The annual hurling championship in September is a major national event. Another, on New Year's Day, is the *Poc Fada*, or Long Stroke, when men vie to see who can strike the *sliotar*, or hurling ball, the greatest distance along a country road. The Millennium celebration in 1999/2000 was marked in Cork by the striking of a burning *sliotar* to kindle a beacon.

Belatedly remembering his nephew, the king rushes forth, fearing the worst for the child, but Setanta stands unharmed over the dead body of the hound. When leapt upon, he had coolly struck his ball right into the dog's throat and killed him instantly. When the host Culainn bemoans the loss of a valuable guard dog, the honourable Setanta volunteers to act as his hound until such time as a replacement can be found. This obligation he duly fulfils, thereby gaining the name *Cú Chulainn*, or the Hound of Culainn. Later he will become known by another and more threatening name, the Hound of Ulster.

CÚCHULAINN'S EDUCATION

Cathbad, the king's senior druid, is responsible for educating Cúchulainn. One morning Cathbad prophesies that a youth who takes up arms on that day will become the most famous warrior in Ireland – although his life will be short. The boy doesn't hesitate but goes to his uncle, King Conor Mac Nessa, demanding a man's weapons. He tests and breaks all those given to him, however, until at last the king brings out his own sword, spear and shield to see if they will prove strong enough for the

Setanta volunteers to act as Culainn's hound, thereby gaining the name of *Cú Chulainn*, or the Hound of Culainn.

demanding child. They are, and Cúchulainn takes possession of them in lordly manner. And as for the warning that his life will be short? 'Little care I,' says he, 'though I were but one day or one night in being, so long as after me the history of myself and my doings may endure.'

That day he gallops out across the plains in the king's chariot, returning in triumph that evening with the bleeding heads of several enemies tied to the shafts. The proud claim that it is better to live a short, glorious life than a long, uneventful one is characteristic of the warlike Celtic culture.

As a young man Cúchulainn is sent for advanced warfare training to the renowned and fearsome warrior-woman Scáthach across the water in Alba (modern Scotland). Scáthach is a terrifying creature who demands much of the young men she accepts in her camp. And what Scáthach doesn't demand, her sister, Aife (the old spelling of the popular name Aoife), takes in the way of pleasure. There is no shortage of women – human or Otherworld – vying for this young hero's affections, although, as befits a warrior, he remains shy and suspicious of female charms. That he is good looking is obvious, with his:

> ... *hundred ringlets of red-gold flaming around his neck, four dimples in each of his two cheeks, seven gems of brilliance in each of his two royal eyes, seven toes on each of his two feet, seven fingers on each of his two hands, with the grasp of a hawk's claws on each of them separately ...*

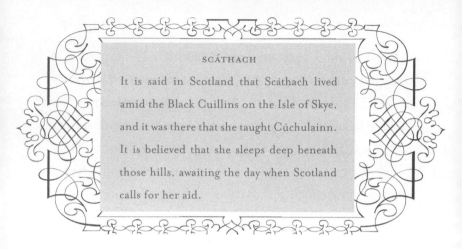

SCÁTHACH

It is said in Scotland that Scáthach lived amid the Black Cuillins on the Isle of Skye, and it was there that she taught Cúchulainn. It is believed that she sleeps deep beneath those hills, awaiting the day when Scotland calls for her aid.

Inevitably, Cúchulainn becomes briefly involved with Aife and when he finally returns to Ireland, having learned all Scáthach can teach him, the other woman is carrying his child. This interlude is to have tragic repercussions later.

CÚCHULAINN'S MAGIC

As a warrior, Cúchulainn develops some amazing skills very similar to the kind we now admire in martial-arts movies. Among these is the 'salmon leap', whereby he can jump from the depth of a river to a high rock, or cross a chasm with a single bound. (This last comes in handy when he has to navigate the ill-tempered bridge to Scáthach's camp, one which bends and bucks whenever anyone sets foot on it, throwing them into the chasm below.)

He also excels at the skill of running on the edge of a moving chariot wheel, or even a shield, while hurling his spear with deadly accuracy. This spear, too, is no ordinary weapon. Given to him by Scáthach as a parting gift, the Gae Bolga is a horrifying instrument of death which is not only hideously barbed, making it impossible to retrieve other than by pulling it right through the victim, but is also an early Celtic guided missile, in that it will follow and strike down its intended prey, no matter how he may dodge or what stands in the way. Aware of its appalling powers, Cúchulainn uses it only in dire straits.

GAE BOLGA

One dreadful occasion on which Cúchulainn uses the Gae Bolga is when Connla, his son by Aife of Alba, comes to Ireland in search of him. Standing on the shore, the child proudly refuses to identify himself, and Cúchulainn is obliged by honour to challenge him to combat. Connla, inheriting his father's characteristics, is already so strong that he can only be killed with the magical spear. Only then do father and son recognise each other and as his child dies, the warrior is heartbroken.

The strangest quality possessed by Cúchulainn is the *ríastrad*, or raging battle frenzy, into which he passes whenever taunted:

> *Then he made a red bowl of his face and his visage on him;*
> *he swallowed one of his two eyes into his head so that a wild*
> *crane could hardly have dragged it from the back of his skull.*
> *The other sprang out until it was on his cheek outside. His*

lips were marvellously contorted … His hair curled round his head like the red branches of a thorn tree in the gap of Atalta … As high, as thick, as strong, as powerful, as long, as the mast of a great ship was the straight stream of dark blood that rose up from the very top of his head so that it made a dark smoke of wizardry like the smoke of a palace when the king comes to equip himself in the evening of a wintry day.

If, in the grip of this rage, Cúchulainn reaches for the dreaded Gae Bolga to wreak his vengeance, the only person who can calm him is his beloved wife, Emer. His wooing of this lovely girl, and the challenges he faced to win her hand, are the subject of legends on their own.

Cúchulainn can jump from the depth of a river to a high rock, or cross a chasm with a single bound.

This natural pass in the mountains, known as the Gap of the North, effectively divides Ulster from the rest of Ireland.

DEFENCE OF THE GAP OF THE NORTH

Cúchulainn is remembered above all for his single-handed defence of the Gap of the North against the marauding forces of Connacht, sent by Queen Maeve to seize the Brown Bull of Cooley. This natural pass in the mountains effectively divides Ulster from the rest of Ireland, and over the centuries it has always allowed just a small number of experienced men to prevent an army advancing into their territory.

But during the battle with Queen Maeve's army, Cúchulainn is forced to defend the Gap all by himself. This is because, at the beginning of every winter, the Red Branch Knights, the fierce fighting men of Ulster, are smitten with agonising pains similar to those of women in childbirth, and they are unable to move, let alone fight, for nine days and nights. The Pangs of Ulster, as they are known, are a curse laid upon them by Macha, a queen of the *sidhe* who marries a mortal, but who is scornfully treated by the king while she herself is in childbirth.

It is fascinating to speculate whether a genuine event lies at the heart of this legend. Was it a specific occasion, lost long ago in the mists of time, when an Ulster fighting clan fell ill with food poisoning or similar? Whatever it was, it was cataclysmic enough to become incorporated into permanent legend as a repeating calamity for Ulstermen. It falls to Cúchulainn – immune to the malady because he was not born in Ulster – to hold the ford across the river at the heart of the pass.

Here he stands on a rock in the midst of the water, challenging every Connacht warrior to single-handed combat. Each one is slain, and the hero himself is also wounded. At one point he is near death and, as his wife Emer tends him, a shining figure approaches. It is his father, Lugh, the sun god, who takes his son to be healed in the Otherworld – a classic example of how worlds intermingle at crucial times. Cúchulainn is tempted to stay in the Land of Youth forever, especially as he is tended by the beautiful Fand, wife of the sea god, Manannán Mac Lir, but eventually his love for Emer and his vow to uphold honour above all else force him to leave. Fearing that Fand's attractions will pull Cúchulainn away from her, Emer asks the druids to brew a drink of forgetfulness, so that his time in the magical land will disappear from his mind. And so, powerful once more, Cúchulainn returns to defend the Gap of the North. This episode is in a tale called *The Sickbed of Cúchulainn*.

Whenever Cúchulainn meets the Mórrígan, goddess of battle, he remembers the prophecy about his life being cut short.

Whenever the warrior meets the Mórrígan, goddess of battle, he remembers the prophecy about his life being cut short. On one occasion, near to the end, he meets an old woman washing bloodstained garments in the river. As he passes by, he recognises the garments as being his own and the washer at the ford as being none other than the bringer of death. But being Cúchulainn, he presses on, eager for glory.

In the end, Queen Maeve resorts to mystical practices to conquer the unconquerable. She commissions three hideous sisters, all trained in the dark arts (did Shakespeare know of this Irish legend when he penned *Macbeth*?). They create confusion in Cúchulainn's mind so that he dashes straight into the heart of Maeve's army, where the Connacht men stab him with his own spear.

Fatally wounded, he staggers to a standing stone and ties himself to it, so that he may remain upright, sword in hand, fighting to the last. It is only when the Mórrígan, in the shape of a raven, perches on the shoulder of the dying hero that his opponents dare to approach – and even then, with one last spasm, Cúchulainn slices the arm off the first man to touch him, before he breathes his last and is beheaded.

A bronze statue in the General Post Office on Dublin's O'Connell Street commemorates this dramatic end to a hero's life. But near Knockbridge crossroads in Co. Louth, an ancient monolith known either as Cúchulainn's Stone or Clochafarmore – the Stone of the Big Man – can still be seen. Cattle, perhaps the descendants of the Brown Bull of Cooley, often graze around its grey bulk and, from time to time, ravens perch on it.

Cúchulainn's Stone, Co. Louth:
the site in legend of a heroic death.

Fionn Mac Cumhaill

If Cúchulainn represents the glory of young man-hood in battle, then Fionn Mac Cumhaill, with his brave band of Fianna, calls to those who love the beauty of forest and mountainside. The Fianna, heroes of a thousand legends, were a band who, like the Red Branch Knights, were sworn to guard their king at Tara and their country against all danger. Unlike the Ulster knights, however, these lads, who roamed the countryside from Kerry in the south to Donegal in the north, were far more at home climbing the hills, hunting in the woods, and cooking supper over an open fire than drinking from fine silver goblets and boasting in royal banqueting halls. The Fianna are in tune with the natural world, and none more so than Fionn himself.

In legend, Fionn Mac Cumhaill is said to have created the Giant's Causeway, Co. Antrim.

BIRTH AND CHILDHOOD

Fionn's mortal father is Cumhall, leader of the Fianna, while his mother, Muirne, is daughter of the druid Tadg Mac Nuadha, son of Nuadha of the Tuatha Dé Danann. Here again legend gives us a miraculous child with parentage from both this and the Otherworld. When Cumhall is killed by those eager to take over the leadership, the baby is adopted by two wise old druidesses and taken into hiding amid the deep forests of the Slieve Bloom mountains. Here the child, named Fionn for his fair hair, grows strong enough to seek his destiny – vengeance for his father and leadership of the Fianna.

Fionn heads for Tara, seat of the High King Cormac Mac Airt (recruiting his father's loyal followers on the way, and retrieving the bag of crane skin that holds the magic of the Fianna). He demands to be accepted; at first the king is doubtful, but when Fionn successfully slays a terrifying monster who attacks Tara every Samhain, his future is assured.

Red Branch Knights may have assessed their status by the number of bloody heads they hung in the Trophy Hall at Emain Macha, but it wasn't enough in the Fianna to be a fierce fighter. They prized learning too, the art of poetry, knowledge of the old ways and the old tales, and, above all, wisdom. To acquire the formidable intellectual skills expected of a leader, Fionn seeks the wisest of the old druids, Finegas, who has been living in seclusion as a hermit on the banks of the Boyne River for many years, waiting in patience to catch the Salmon of Knowledge and thus acquire all the wisdom of both this and the Otherworld.

The Salmon of Knowledge is a recurrent theme and a much-loved image throughout Irish legend. It spends its life in the River Boyne and feeds on the nuts that drop from the nine magic hazel trees of wisdom growing around the sacred pool at the river's source. The pool is not to be found by mortal men, but someone fortunate enough to catch and eat the salmon will receive the gift of all knowledge and understanding.

The story of how Fionn acquired his legendary wisdom is a good one, demonstrating as the best tales always do how the obvious path is not always the right one. On the very day he is accepted by Finegas as a student, the old druid at last manages to catch the Salmon of Knowledge. Delighted, he sets it to cook over a fire of twigs, and then goes off to offer thanksgiving rituals, leaving Fionn in charge of the fish with strict instructions not to eat the tiniest scrap.

The Salmon of Knowledge is a recurrent theme and a much-loved image throughout Irish legend.

Fionn has no intention of disobeying his revered master and diligently turns the fish to ensure its even cooking, burning his thumb in the process. Without thinking, Fionn puts the burnt thumb in his mouth, tastes the salmon, and the gift of knowledge is transferred. When Finegas comes back, he knows immediately what has happened. However, being a wise old druid, he realises that this was fated and sends Fionn off with his blessing, after which, we hope, he enjoys a peaceful and contented old age. And as for Fionn? Whenever he is in need of good counsel, he simply puts his thumb in his mouth and the right answer comes to him.

THE GIFT OF POETRY

Fionn is not only strong and wise but also gifted in poetry, especially that celebrating the beauty of the Irish landscape. There are many ancient poems attributed to the hero himself, such as this, translated by TW Rolleston:

The Song of Fionn in Praise of May

May Day! delightful day!
Bright colours play the vales along.
Now wakes at morning's slender ray,
Wild and gay, the blackbird's song.
Now comes the bird of dusty hue,
The loud cuckoo, the summer-lover;
Branching trees are thick with leaves …

Many are the battles Fionn and the Fianna fight, many their victories. Young men everywhere yearn to join their elite ranks but few are accepted. The initiation tests are severe: among them, the ability to stand in a deep hole in the ground and defend yourself with only a staff against ten warriors throwing spears; to run at full speed through a dense thicket without catching a single hair on a branch; taking a thorn out of your foot without slowing down or allowing any of your pursuers to come near you.

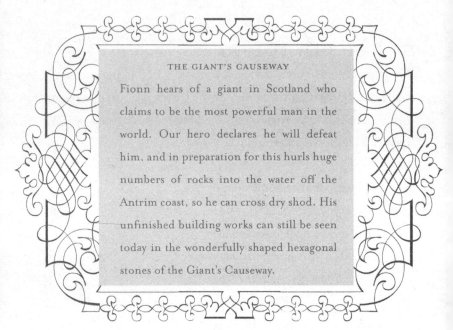

THE GIANT'S CAUSEWAY

Fionn hears of a giant in Scotland who claims to be the most powerful man in the world. Our hero declares he will defeat him, and in preparation for this hurls huge numbers of rocks into the water off the Antrim coast, so he can cross dry shod. His unfinished building works can still be seen today in the wonderfully shaped hexagonal stones of the Giant's Causeway.

When not fighting battles, Fionn enjoys hunting with his two loyal wolfhounds, Bran and Sceolan, who lead him to his first great love, Sadbh or Sive. One day they are pursuing a beautiful deer, but having cornered it, they don't attack. Rather, they fawn delightedly on it, then lie down to protect it. Fionn realises that this must be one of the Good People in disguise, so he takes it in safety to his fort on the Hill of Allen (a fairy hill, and so itself a place of power). And indeed the deer turns out to be Sive, a goddess transformed by an evil druid whose advances she had scorned. She can only regain her true form while within Fionn's fort. They marry and live happily until one day, while Fionn is absent, the druid tricks her into coming outside the fort, whereupon she is changed back into a deer and vanishes. Broken-hearted, Fionn searches high and low, but although he never finds Sive again, he does discover their child, Oisín, hidden by her in a cave.

124

OISÍN AND TÍR NA NÓG

Oisín grows up to become a great poet and is beloved by all who set eyes on him. One day, as he rides with his companions over the mountains above the lakes of Killarney, Niamh of the Golden Hair appears through a magical mist from Lough Leane on a white horse and cajoles Oisín into visiting Tír na nÓg with her. Of course the few days he spends in her company are really hundreds of years. When – in a touching incident comparing the glittering, never-ending glories of the Otherworld with a sudden memory of the scent of real earth, water and grass in Ireland – he finally persuades Niamh to let him come back on a brief visit to see his friends, he finds everything changed, his comrades long gone. Leaning from his horse to help some workmen lift a huge stone, he falls to the ground and is instantly an old, old man who dies before their eyes.

Oisín fell in love with Niamh of the Golden Hair at Lough Leane.

ETERNAL TRIANGLE: FIONN, GRÁINNE AND DIARMUID

Unlike Cúchulainn, Fionn does live to a ripe old age, and thereby hangs another tale. The High King, Cormac Mac Airt, wishes to honour Fionn's life of achievement and offers him his young daughter, Gráinne, in marriage. But when Gráinne looks at Fionn she sees not a hero, but merely a grey-haired old man. Worse still, at the celebratory feast of their marriage, she first sets eyes on a tall, handsome youth named Diarmuid, one of Fionn's loyal warriors. She falls in love and pleads with Diarmuid to flee with her. An honourable man, he refuses. But then Gráinne uses a stronger persuasion – not tears or cajoling, but the dreaded *geasa* or compulsion. This is a recognised form of pressure within the Celtic world, put upon one individual by another, with which they must comply, whether they like it or not. Put under *geasa* by Gráinne, Diarmuid can do nothing but run away with her. Noble to the end, however, he says that he will not make love to her until such time as Fionn forgives them and they are free to marry.

That doesn't seem very likely as the ageing Fionn is furious beyond measure. He pursues the young couple the length and breadth of the country, so that they cannot rise in the morning where they lie down to sleep the night before, and cannot leave a house by the same door as the one where they entered. Today you will find rocks, hillsides, cromlechs and caves everywhere in Ireland named the Bed of Diarmuid and Gráinne (often regarded as powerful fertility sites). In the end, however, Fionn realises what a fool he must look, relents, and the lovers, at last, live happily ever after.

Today you will find rocks, hillsides, cromlechs and caves everywhere in Ireland named the Bed of Diarmuid and Gráinne.

Well, not quite. In that curious twist of fate so characteristic of Celtic legend, Diarmuid and Fionn are out hunting together one day, many years later, and Diarmuid is fatally injured by a wild boar. Fionn tries to help him, but the younger man dies. The broken-hearted Gráinne accuses Fionn of his murder and vows to bring up her children to scorn his name. Nevertheless, as time goes on, she starts to believe in his innocence. In the end, she marries Fionn and takes her rightful place in society once more.

Legend and folklore hold firmly that Fionn Mac Cumhaill himself never died – that he is still alive today. He and the Fianna sleep in a hidden cave in a secret valley in the mountains, awaiting the day when Ireland shall have need of them again. Lying quietly at his feet, as they did after many a day's exhausting hunting in the hills, are his hounds, Bran and Sceolan.

One popular folktale tells of a child who finds his way by accident into that secret cave and sees the sleeping warrior giants.

'Is it time?' asks one huge figure as he raises his head. The child has presence of mind. 'Not yet,' he replies, and the figure returns to sleep as the young intruder flees.

CÚCHULAINN AND FIONN MAC CUMHAILL: THE ORIGIN OF THEIR LEGEND

Two superhuman warriors, half gods, half men. One seeking honour and victory in battle, the other a lover of nature and poetry. One delighting in the riotous gatherings of the drinking hall and the blast of the battle trumpets, his counterpart preferring the company of quiet companions and hounds by peaceful camp fires. You could even see them as alter egos of the same individual – the warlike figure who at the end of the day wanders home to walk his dog – but it goes deeper than that.

It is possible that the romantic tales of Fionn and the Fianna – told mainly in verse – come from the older settlers, the gentle Fir Bolg, instinctive lovers of the land and the soil, worshippers of the old nature gods, still living secretly amid the woods and boglands of the south and passing down their stories of past heroes around the fire. In contrast, the bloodthirsty stories of the Ulster Cycle – recounted principally in prose – arise from the warlike world of the Celts and the ruling classes of the north, when Conor Mac Nessa held the High Kingship, where tales of courage were taught to the boy troops who wished to be Red Branch Knights and hero-warriors themselves one day.

Lia Fáil, or Stone of Destiny, stands on top of the Hill of Tara, Co. Meath.

Part Two

Nature and the Otherworld

SACRED PLACES, MAGICAL

CREATURES AND THE

TURNING YEAR

The dangers of the unpredictable ocean were familiar to our ancestors.

The Lore of the Sea

We're a small enough island here on the westernmost edge of Europe – no more than 300 miles at our longest point, and 189 miles at the widest. Our coastline though, deeply indented by the ceaseless attack of the Atlantic waves, is more than 3,500 miles in length. Those who live by the sea know it as an integral, inescapable part of everyday life. Food has always been gathered here, wreckage collected, journeys commenced, traders welcomed, invaders fearfully glimpsed.

For thousands of years the sea was the natural highway, the simplest and quickest way from one point on the coast to another. In *The Voyage of Mael Duin*, the hero (on the west coast) is searching for the killers of his father, and he is told that they are in Leix, over on the east side of the country: 'And he asked the way to wend to Leix, and the guides told him that he could only go by sea ...'

Until the middle of the 20th century, small commercial boats traded up and down the shores of Ireland, transporting goods, mail and passengers between communities, much as they still do today in the fjordland of Norway. What would take hours of winding in and out along the roads of Connemara or Sligo takes no time at all in a boat. Young men in Antrim still cheerfully head up to the island of Islay or the Mull of Kintyre in Scotland for a party, a distance of 12 miles or less, while they might not consider going inland the same distance.

SEAFARING CUSTOMS

The dangers of the unpredictable ocean were familiar to our ancestors. Few families would escape losing one or more members in a fishing accident, a cliff fall, an error of judgement in gathering seaweed at low tide. Many of the beliefs and customs that grew up around trying to stay safe near the sea are still observed in coastal communities today.

If you meet a red-haired woman on your way to a day's fishing, for example, it is a sign of bad luck, and you should turn for home. A fox crossing your path gives the same warning. When launching the boats of a fishing fleet, three should never go out at the same time. (For this reason, two are often lashed together and launched as one.) On board you should never whistle, nor mention a pig or a priest. Any of these could annoy pagan sea spirits who are listening unseen, and might unleash their anger, with disastrous results.

The traditional currach is lightweight and easy to launch.

The sea is the kingdom of Manannán Mac Lir, god of the ocean, but he is seldom seen. It is more often the Good People – themselves keen fishermen – who might be scudding by in their own boats. If you do see them, it can be a friendly warning that bad weather is on the way and it is advisable to turn and row for the shore as quickly as possible. There are stories of fairy boats challenging fishermen to a race, only to disappear as harbour is safely reached, while a sudden storm blows up that would have sunk them if they had remained out.

There are many stories too of phantom currachs, ghostly boats that appear silently out of the darkness as fishermen pull in their nets at night. Often they contain a crew of drowned men. It is a warning that anyone who sees them should go home and put his affairs in order, for he will be joining them soon. There was even a long-held belief that you should never save a drowning man, for to do so would be to thwart the sea's wishes, and 'the sea must have its due'.

That the ocean is dangerous, unpredictable and merciless is evidenced by the legends, stories, beliefs and customs that permeate the lives of all shore dwellers in Ireland. The resignation in the final words of old Maurya in Synge's classic *Riders to the Sea* must have been felt by many Irishwomen over the centuries:

> *They're all gone now, and there isn't anything more the sea can do to me ... I'll have no call now to be up crying and praying when the wind breaks from the south, and you can hear the surf is in the east, and the surf is in the west, making a great stir ...*

THE GREAT WAVES OF IRELAND

Throughout history special individual waves have been recognised that bear their own characteristics.

For example, Tuile Ladrann, or the Flood of Ladru, off the Sligo/Mayo coast was known in the Middle Ages as one of 'the great waves of Ireland'.

On the peninsula of Iveragh in south Kerry there is a traditional belief regarding a sunken city under the Wave of Toim, which rises and falls just outside Rossbeigh.

Glandore in West Cork, where Cliona can be heard mourning her lost love.

The little harbour of Glandore in West Cork is home to Cliona's Wave. According to legend, Cliona, one of the daughters of the sea god Manannán Mac Lir, fell in love with a human and chose the mortal life so that she could be with him. However, one afternoon as she lay sleeping on the cliffs at Glandore, the sea rose and took her back, sweeping her away from her lover forever and back to Manannán's kingdom. Ever since then, she can be heard mourning her lost love in this special wave, which echoes and cries through sea caves below the cliffs. It's an eerie sound.

To venture out too far is to quit this land altogether, and beyond the Ninth Wave is foreign territory, beyond Ireland's influence. This was why the Tuatha Dé Danann asked the invading Celts to retreat 'beyond the Ninth Wave'. Once they were

To voyage beyond the Ninth
Wave is to leave all that is familiar.

outside Ireland's environment, enveloping mists could be raised,
enchantments set about the island to protect it.

To voyage beyond the Ninth Wave is to leave all that is familiar.
It was, in ancient times, a punishment for severe crime. Set adrift
in a small boat without oars or sail, and with only a limited supply
of fresh water, you were at the mercy of the gods, who would
decide what should be done with you.

FAIRY ISLANDS

There are magical islands off our coastline, places that are seen
but rarely by human beings.

Chief of these is Hy Brasil, which can be glimpsed at sunset,
floating on the horizon between sea and sky. Some say it only
appears every seven years; others that it makes itself visible any
time to those with the eyes to see beyond the veil. But all are
agreed that it is an island of beauty and happiness, where there is
no ageing or sickness or unhappiness, where everyone lives happily ever after. Tír na nÓg, which is everywhere and yet invisible,
under the hills, within a fairy fort, in a lake, can also be on this
enchanted island.

Hy Brasil is also known as Moy Mell, the Plain of Honey,
and as one of the Isles of the Blest. It was actually marked on

maps right up to the 19th century. One 17th-century sea captain claimed to have landed on the island, where he found a strange enchanter living alone in a stone castle, along with many huge black rabbits. (Rabbits were introduced by the Normans in the 12th century, so they may have been rabbits or a variant form of the Irish hare. Or, given that it was Hy Brasil, perhaps they weren't animals at all but residents skilled in magic, disguising themselves from uninvited visitors.)

Donegal, Mayo, Galway, Kerry and Cork all claim ownership of this sought-after isle. People have sworn that they have seen Hy Brasil at evening, just as the sun is setting, describing in fascinating detail the little fields, cattle grazing, trees laden with fruit. There is a tradition that if you can land and light a fire, the enchantment will be broken and the island will remain in our world from then on.

People have sworn that they have seen Hy Brasil at evening, just as the sun is setting.

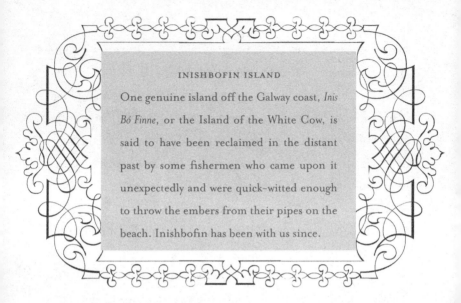

INISHBOFIN ISLAND

One genuine island off the Galway coast, *Inis Bó Finne*, or the Island of the White Cow, is said to have been reclaimed in the distant past by some fishermen who came upon it unexpectedly and were quick-witted enough to throw the embers from their pipes on the beach. Inishbofin has been with us since.

Tradition speaks also of an *oileán sidheanta*, or fairy island, which can sometimes be seen off Rossan Point in Co. Donegal. It is said to emerge from the water just before sunrise on a May morning every seven years, complete with trees, cattle, hedgerows and laneways. On one such occasion a number of men set out in a boat, bringing a pot of red embers with them to disenchant it. They saw a girl sitting underneath a tree, knitting. Immediately she threw her ball of yarn into the boat and it stuck there, tying the craft to the mysterious island. The boat began to shake violently and one of the men, afraid for his life, burned through the thread with an ember. Immediately the island sank into the sea, and the men lost their chance.

Arainn Bheag, or Little Aran, is said to lie west of the geographical Aran Islands and to surface every seven years around midwinter. Roderick O'Flaherty wrote in 1684 of one Muircheartach

O Laoi, who was abducted to this secret isle and only effected his escape after some time. He managed to take away with him a magical book, from which he learned incredible medical skills. Could this be yet another folk memory of learned druidic texts, long since lost?

Cill Stuifin, off Liscannor Bay in Co. Clare, is said to have been magically concealed by a druid going off to war. Unfortunately, he was killed in the battle, and since nobody else had his power or knew his magic formula, Cill Stuifin remains hidden to mortal eyes. Discovering unusual or inexplicable wreckage on the sea-shore, however, is taken as continuing proof that the truth is out there, somewhere. The key is believed by some to lie hidden in a lake on Slieve Callan, but naturally enough the specific lake is not identified.

TRAVELLING FAR: *IMMRAMA*

Setting out to find the Isles of the Blest was a challenge seized upon by many heroes in Celtic legend. These travel tales are accorded a special division of their own in mythology, *immrama*. The term, which literally means 'rowing about', covers such wonderful voyages as those of Bran, Mael Duin, Ui Chorra, and Snedgus and Mac Riagla. The later *Voyage of St Brendan* could also be said to belong to this category, although in all likelihood it was put together with material from the earlier stories.

In all the tales, the hero sets out on a quest across the ocean – always to the west, since Ireland was then at the westernmost edge of the known world – either to fulfil his destiny or to discover and explore fabled locations. The adventures he encounters on

In all the tales, the hero sets out on a quest across the ocean — always to the west, since Ireland was then at the westernmost edge of the known world.

the way, and the delights or terrors awaiting him on the various islands, make exciting reading even today, and they must have been listened to breathlessly in the halls of earlier times. Because they were written down by Christian monks, inevitably religious themes are inserted into the texts, but in most instances this is very obviously done, rather as new brickwork shows up on the restoration of an ancient building.

In *The Voyage of Bran*, for example, there is a strange maiden who appears unexpectedly in the hero's feasting hall and sings of the beauty of the Otherworld islands, which are peopled only by women whose sole aim it is to please the traveller:

> *Many-shaped Emne by the sea,*
> *Whether it be near, whether it be far,*
> *In which are many thousands of motley women,*
> *Which the clear sea encircles.*
> *If he has heard the voice of the music,*
> *The chorus of the little birds from Imchiuin,*
> *A small band of women will come from a height,*
> *To the plain of sport in which he is …*

This is, however, rather abruptly followed by a Christian passage:

> *A great birth will come in after ages,*
> *That will not be in a lofty place,*
> *The son of a woman whose mate will not be known.*
> *He will seize the rule of the many thousands,*
> *A rule without beginning, without end,*
> *He has created the world so that it is perfect,*
> *Whose are earth and sea,*
> *Woe to him that shall be under His unwill!*
> *'Tis He that made the heavens,*
> *Happy he that has a white heart,*
> *He will purify hosts under pure water,*
> *'Tis He that will heal your sicknesses …*

At this point in the poem, the mysterious visitor is allowed to return to the questionable topic (to monastic eyes!) of willing women:

> *Not to all of you is my speech,*
> *Though its great marvel has been made known.*
> *Let Bran hear from the crowd of the world,*
> *What of wisdom has been told to him.*
> *Do not fall on a bed of sloth,*
> *Let not thy intoxication overcome thee,*
> *Begin a voyage across the clear sea,*
> *If perchance thou mayst reach the land of women.*

One can visualise the monk, bent over his desk, laboriously transcribing the legend, raising shocked eyebrows, and fetching one of his superiors to advise on the insertion of suitably Christian imagery to counter the dangerous idea of the land of women.

Bran, of course, can't resist such temptation and when the fair visitor disappears as abruptly as she arrived, he collects a crew (the magical formula of nine times nine men) and sets off in search of adventure. Once at sea, they have an encounter with none other than Manannán Mac Lir himself, who gives a wonderful description of the hidden land beneath the waves:

> *Along the top of a wood has swum*
> *Thy coracle across ridges,*
> *There is a wood of beautiful fruit*
> *Underneath the prow of thy little skiff …*

Bran has many adventures with his crew, but when they return home, one man jumps ashore and is immediately reduced to dust. Bran realises that they have been away for several centuries and can never set foot in Ireland again. He calls out the story of their voyage to those on shore, so that it may be written down for future generations, and then sets sail to the west once more, never to be seen again.

The Voyage of Mael Duin is filled with fascinating details, including a paradise of birds, an island of sheep, fiery volcanic eruptions, an encounter with an iceberg and a mysterious palace guarded by a tiny cat:

When their mouths and their noses were full of the stench of the sea, they sighted an island which was not large, and therein a fort surrounded by a white, high rampart as if it were built of burnt lime, or as if it were all one rock of chalk. Great was its height from the sea: it all but reached the clouds. The fort was open wide. Round the rampart were great, snow-white houses. When they entered the largest of these they saw no-one there, save a small cat which was in the midst of the house playing on the four stone pillars that were there. It was leaping, from each pillar to the other. It looked a little at the men, and did not stop itself from its play. After that, they saw three rows on the wall of the house round about, from one door post to the other. A row there, first, of brooches of gold and of silver, with their pins in the wall, and a row of neck-torques of gold and of silver: like hoops of a vat was each of them. The third row of great swords, with hilts of gold and of silver. The rooms were full of white quilts and shining garments. A roasted ox moreover, and a flitch in the midst of the house, and great vessels with good intoxicating liquor. 'Hath this been left for us?' saith Mael Duin to the cat. It looked at him suddenly and began to play again. Then Mael Duin realised it was for them that the dinner had been left.

When one of the crew tries to steal a necklace, however, he is immediately burned to ashes by the little cat, necessitating tactful action by Mael Duin, who:

... soothed the cat with his words, and set the necklace in its place and cleansed the ashes from the floor of the enclosure, and cast them on the shore of the sea.

The well-known *Voyage of St Brendan* was undoubtedly put together using much of the detail from earlier *immrama* (it features icebergs and islands of birds and sheep), but it also displays an engaging knowledge of both the local Kerry landscape and the craft of boatbuilding:

Having received the blessing of this holy father and all his monks, he proceeded to the remotest part of his own country, where his parents abode. However, he willed not to visit them, but went up to the summit of the mountain there, which extends into the ocean, on which is 'St Brendan's Seat', and there he fitted up a tent, near a narrow creek, where a boat could enter. Then St Brendan and his companions, using iron implements, prepared a light vessel with wicker sides and ribs, such as is usually made in that country, and covered it with cow-hide, tanned in oak-bark, tarring the joints thereof, and put on board provisions for 40 days, with butter enough to dress hides for covering the boat, and all utensils needed for the use of the crew.

It was such rare factual detail that inspired Tim Severin and his crew to undertake their own *immram* in 1976, building a boat to exactly the same specifications as St Brendan's. They undertook a challenging voyage via the Hebrides, the Faroes and Iceland, eventually reaching the coast of North America at Newfoundland. What Tim wanted to show was not so much that it *had* been done by St Brendan, but that it *could* be done.

The ancient Irish were enthusiastic travellers, as indeed they had to be. They were certainly familiar with the coast of Scotland and the Hebrides, probably the Orkneys and Shetland, and the lower reaches of Scandinavia. To the south, there was trade with Spain and France, and visitors from the Mediterranean and the Norselands had been coming to our shores since ancient times. Whether learned from traders or experienced at first hand, the descriptions in the *immrama* are certainly based on fact, however they may have been embroidered for the purposes of storytelling.

To the listener in early Celtic Ireland, hearing such tales of adventure must have been awe-inspiring, unforgettable. After all, someone who had never seen a volcano or an iceberg might well regard such phenomena as magic. The stories tell us a great deal too, though, about the body of travel knowledge readily available in ancient Ireland. Clearly we cannot assume with smug confidence that our ancestors went nowhere, knew nothing, were totally ignorant of the wider world. That was far from being the case.

The ancient Irish were enthusiastic travellers, as indeed they had to be.

SKELLIG: LAST OUTPOST OF THE ANCIENT WISDOM?

The Isles of the Blest should not be visited if you ever want to return to this world again. There is one island, though, that can be visited, and it may hold more secrets of the old ways than we can imagine. Great Skellig, a looming black rock rising high above the crashing Atlantic waves, is clearly visible from the Kerry coast, but you will nevertheless have to wait until the experienced local boatmen deem time and tide propitious for the risky crossing.

When that day dawns at last, you will also need strong nerves and considerable energy. Most of the offshore islands around the Irish coast are flat and friendly places, little green fields stretching to sandy beaches where seals loll at ease and sheep graze peacefully in the dunes. But not Skellig. This is a majestic, frightening place, one that offers no welcome, and, indeed, seems to threaten intruders.

The boat journey takes a scary three quarters of an hour. Imagine what a sea crossing was like in ancient times, in a fragile coracle, or curragh. The seabirds and clouds sweep across the sky above, just as they did when other pilgrims made this hazardous journey long ago.

People – warriors, wise women, seekers after answers – have been coming to Skellig since time immemorial. The great Celtic warrior Ir was brought here for burial after he drowned attempting to land and wrest Ireland from the Tuatha Dé Danann. Sheer, savage rocks in the Atlantic are not the easiest place to bury anyone, so the site's magical power and high status must have been great indeed, when that tale was first told. It was able to offer safe haven too: In the 5th century, Duagh, king of West Munster, fled here from a battle, indicating a sacred site or sanctuary. By the 8th century, a Christian monastery had been established on the rock, and it is the remains of this that are most visible in Skellig today.

From the landing place, an endless flight of crumbling stone steps leads upward, one narrow strip of (fairly) firm reality bordered by little but a treacherous slope and a vertical drop. Sea pinks offer a welcome splash of colour in this grey and black world, while puffins actually nest underneath Skellig's steps, peeping out to stare at the climbers. It's a terrifying yet utterly beautiful place.

Arriving at the monks' cells and gazing out, breathless, over the sparkling sea beyond, one's first reaction is bewilderment. Why establish a monastery here? A hermitage, yes, that would be understandable. Holy men and women have ever sought throughout the ages for the most remote place possible in which to come closer to the world of the mind. But a

Puffins nest underneath Skellig's steps, peeping out to stare at the climbers.

149

monastery is usually founded where there are fields and rivers and people to support it. Postulants for the cloisters, servants to look after the flocks and herds that feed the monks, craftsmen within reach to supply vellum, inks, cloth and more. On this wild Atlantic outpost, landing is not possible for half the year, and storms can cut off contact with the mainland for weeks at a time. Even carrying up supplies from a small boat would be a major undertaking.

But a monastery was established here for two key reasons. First is the popularity of the saint under whose patronage Skellig is now firmly established: St Michael, who fought and conquered the devil. Second, a 13th-century German source records that Skellig was the spot where St Patrick finally banished the last serpents from Ireland. Here we have two clear links between the old pagan beliefs and the newer Christian religion.

And the archaeological remains of pre-Christian settlement are there too, though not easy to find. Far up the crags, well beyond the beehive huts, are the remains of a prehistoric enclosure, similar to others built all around the coast of the Dingle peninsula as well as on the neighbouring Blasket Islands. It is probable that when the first company of Christian monks landed here, they moved into existing structures before setting to the task of building their own. Today you have only to shelter momentarily from the icy wind behind one of these ancient walls to share the relief they must have felt.

Recently, and most excitingly, some flights of steps have been discovered that were hewn into the rocks long before the arrival of the monks, which lends a material aspect to what is already

Skellig was the spot where St Patrick finally banished the last serpents from Ireland.

known from legend, folklore and ancient record. If you're wondering why it took so long to find these older steps, then pause to consider the kind of setting we're talking about. Access to any part of Skellig is difficult, and close examination of the wave-lashed seaward sides is rarely feasible, and then only with a very experienced boatman in charge. For detailed, close-up inspection, specialised climbing equipment and more than a dash of insanity are necessary. Skellig is emphatically not the sort of place where you potter peaceably along the waterline, carrying binoculars and notebook.

Lady Wilde, who in her collection of old Irish legends considered these rocks to be 'of great sanctity', described the interesting tradition for young people up to the 19th century of 'going to the Skelligs':

As marriages were not allowed in Lent, it was a custom for the young people of both sexes to make a pilgrimage to the Skellig Rocks during the last Lenten week. A procession was formed of the young girls and bachelors, and tar-barrels were lighted to guide them on the dangerous paths. The idea was to spend the week in prayer, penance and lamentation; the girls praying for good husbands, the bachelors repenting of their sins. But the proceedings gradually degenerated into such a mad carnival of dancing, drinking and fun that the priests denounced the pilgrimage and forbade the annual migration to the Skelligs. Still the practice was continued until the police had orders to clear the rocks. Thus ended the ancient custom of 'going to the Skelligs', for the mayor having pronounced judgement over the usage as 'subversive of all morality and decorum', it was entirely discontinued; and the wild fun and frolic of the Skelligs is now but a tradition preserved in the memory of the oldest inhabitant.

This points to the tradition of a spring pilgrimage to a sacred site, probably linked to Imbolc or the spring equinox, and this in turn adds to the probability that the great pinnacle of rock rising from the sea has been an important ritual centre from early times. Given its remote location, perhaps it was even the site of a druidic centre where wisdom was gained through fasting and separation?

Skellig is, in fact, the westernmost point of an ancient line of power centres known as the Apollo Axis. This line threads its way from Palestine through Delos, Athens and Delphi in Greece, Monte Gargano and Perugia in modern Italy, Bourges and Mont St Michel in France, and St Michael's Mount in Cornwall, ending here on the sheer black cliffs of Skellig Michael in the Atlantic, the end of the known world. These sites are all links in a chain of energy, each a strong power centre where believers could address the gods. Not surprising then that early Christian missionaries, looking ruefully at the stormy seas and the vertiginous rocky heights, took over three of the island sites off the coasts of France, England and Ireland, and firmly dedicated them to the uncompromising saint.

Of the thousands who make the uncomfortable crossing from the mainland to experience Skellig Michael's demanding climbs and dizzying pinnacles, some may come for religious reasons, others for the fascination of a remote and historic settlement. Whatever their reason, they are drawn by a power they cannot identify and cannot explain. As George Bernard Shaw said when he visited in 1910, the Skellig has magic that 'takes you out, far out, of this time and this world'.

Great Skellig, a black rock rising high above the crashing Atlantic waves, is clearly visible from the Kerry coast.

Spirits of the Running Water

esh water is the essence of life, for humans, animals and the land, and our ancestors certainly respected the spirits or deities that inhabited it. Springs, streams, rivers and lakes all have their place in our beliefs and legends, recognised not only as sources of goodness and fertility but as entrances to the Otherworld itself.

SACRED WELLS

To see water bubbling up from the ground, falling from a rocky cleft or emerging from a gap in the mountainside is to experience the magic of nature. In Sligo, a man leads his children down a little lane and bathes their eyes at the small pool half hidden in the undergrowth. On a cliff-top in Waterford, dozens are kneeling in prayer by an old well while others circle the surrounding ruined walls, pausing at intervals to scrape crosses into specific stones. Deep in the West Cork woods, a lone figure is twisting a scrap of cloth around a thorn tree, already laden with offerings, which bends over a bubbling spring. Everywhere in Ireland you will find sacred wells still revered and honoured, sought in times of need and importuned for favours. It's a tradition that has never gone away.

Everywhere in Ireland you will find sacred wells still revered and honoured.

No-one is quite sure just how many holy wells there are in Ireland, but a conservative estimate is at least 3,000. Some are almost forgotten today, overgrown, rarely visited. Others are tourist attractions, with special festival days and ritual observances. Such festivals are now conducted under the banner of Christianity, but the beliefs that spur the faithful to attend are older and more deeply rooted than that.

The key characteristic of our sacred wells is that they are natural springs, bubbling up freely from the earth. Their power lies in the fact that, like rivers and lakes (and indeed the fairy thorn), they have chosen to manifest themselves in this particular place and no other. Human devotees may construct a little sheltering hut or enclosing wall and keep the surroundings clean and neat, but the water supply itself is completely the gift of nature and its deities.

In the pagan world, water is always under the protection of a female spirit. Later, Christianity would rename many wells, rivers and lakes after their own male saints, such as St Patrick or, as in Ardmore, St Declan, in a determined drive to break the old goddess-based religion. Most of the Tobar Padraigs, or St Patrick's Wells, which are dotted all around the country, certainly bore the name of a goddess in pre-Christian times.

Other sacred wells have kept their female deities, especially if the deity in question has been successfully transformed into a Christian saint. Kildare, always associated strongly with Brigit (and later St Brigid), has not only an ancient well but a new one too, both well patronised. St Gobnait's Well, near Ballyvourney in Co. Cork, is dedicated to a Christian saint yet is surrounded by older monuments, including a prehistoric burial mound and a pagan *sheela-na-gig* (or rudimentary female fertility figure) built into the wall of a ruined church. Interestingly, the saint is said to have been led by white deer to this spot, and deer are patterned on the gates to the old churchyard. Deer, and especially white ones, frequently appear in legends as spirits in a shape-shifting disguise.

If a tree grows over the well, that, too, is sacred, and is hung with offerings and petitions – a rag of bright cloth, a twist of yarn, a medal or other token deeply significant to the donor. Often it is a thorn tree that stands thus gaily decorated, but rowan, hazel and other native species are found too.

Sacred wells are places of healing, both of bodily sickness and mental anguish. There are different springs throughout the country that are resorted to for different ailments. There are several named Tobar na Súl, which are said to heal eye infections. There is a Tooth Well at the Burren in Co. Clare, which probably was popular in the days before dentists. St Attracta's in Roscommon has a row of beautiful egg-like stones laid along the top of the surrounding wall. Women hoping to have children handle these stones before drinking the well water.

> In the pagan world, water is always under
> the protection of a female spirit.

At St Attracta's Well in Roscommon, women hoping for children handle these stones.

THE WELL OF THE TUATHA DÉ DANANN

The druids of old were skilled in healing, especially in times of battle. In the Second Battle of Mag Tuiread, the Fomorians played a cruel trick on the Tuatha Dé Danann.

The Tuatha's well, called *Slaine,* or Health, was filled with magical herbs and could give miraculous cures, even to those near death. But one day Ochtriallach, son of the Fomorian king Indech Mac Dé Domnann, had a brainwave. He suggested that under cover of darkness, every man in their force should bring a stone from the River Drowes to cast into the well. This they did, creating a gigantic cairn that completely blocked the healing well, so that the Tuatha could not revive their fallen comrades. They almost lost the battle because of it but, fortunately, Lugh of the Long Arm slew the dreaded Balor of the Evil Eye and won the day for his people, thereby driving the Fomorians from Ireland.

The cairn said to have been thrown up so treacherously by the Fomorians still stands today in Co. Sligo. Now known rather prosaically as the Heapstone, it's a strangely out-of-place towering grey mound in a quiet, green, rural field. It is classified as an ancient monument, but to date has not been excavated. Who knows what threads of ancient knowledge or history are hidden within its huge bulk? Could there be a well or spring still bubbling underneath? Old legends should never be discounted. They will certainly have changed, been embroidered and extended over the centuries, but sift to the very heart and you will generally find seeds of genuine historical or geographical fact. Tellingly, the local name in Irish for this gigantic cairn is *Fás na hAon Oíche*, or 'Grown in One Night'.

Who hasn't tossed a coin into a wishing well? It's an echo of the pagan belief that an offering to the spirit of the water will bring good luck. The tiny lake island of Gougane Barra had,

The Heapstone Cairn, Co. Sligo:
What lies beneath remains a mystery.

within living memory, a small well into which pilgrims threw coins, as well as an overhanging tree that gradually became covered with coins hammered into its bark. (There are similar 'money trees' in other parts of the country: for example, a well-metalled sycamore at Clonenagh in Co. Laois.) That at Gougane was eventually considered too pagan by the clergy, the tiny water source filled in, and the tree removed. Next, a nearby wooden cross became the focus of coin placement. That too was removed, when it was so heavy with metal that it was disintegrating. Finally a firm, no-nonsense well in good modern stonework was constructed at the entrance to the causeway leading to the island, and a sharp notice posted alongside, requesting that the faithful desist from sullying the water and put their donations into the collecting box provided instead. The coins still gleam as brightly as ever in the water of the new well, proof that the old convictions are just too strong.

At Gougane, a wooden cross became the focus of coin placement.

Because sacred wells are entrances to the Otherworld, they can also supply answers to urgent questions. Brigid's Well at Liscannor in Co. Clare is underground and said to have a magical fish living within its waters. If you are fortunate enough to catch a glimpse, even of its tail, then you are sure of getting your wish. This belief is probably related to the most famous spring of Celtic legend, the Well of Wisdom, held by some to be at the source of the Boyne, by others at the source of the Shannon.

THE GREAT RIVERS

Before roads became common, journeys across Ireland meant either following faint paths over high ground or dangerous bogland, or using the rivers as routeways. People travelled in small coracles or currachs along the Shannon, the Nore, the Boyne and the Barrow, indeed any waterway that linked inland settlements with the ocean beyond. Traders and invaders alike also found these rivers ideal for penetrating the country. The abbots of Clonmacnoise on the banks of the Shannon must have questioned the wisdom of its location more than once, when the Vikings came a-raiding.

Great rivers each had their own goddess. Boann ruled the River Boyne, Sinann the Shannon, Lifé the Liffey. The River Lee in Co. Cork had an older name of Ercre, and the island of Gougane Barra at its source was once known as Inis Ercre, or the island of that goddess. There is a river Bride, dedicated to the goddess Brigit, in every county, and sometimes several, showing the love and respect in which she is everywhere held.

Often the origin of the river – the Boyne and the Shannon, to name two – is explained by a folktale in which a forgetful spirit omits to cover the sacred well at night, and it overflows, flooding the landscape and becoming a mighty river. Perhaps this explains Brú na Bóinne, or Palace of the Boyne, one of the most important prehistoric megalithic sites in Europe. It contains the passage graves of Newgrange, Knowth and Dowth, each standing on its own ridge above a bend in the river. The sites are almost completely surrounded by water.

While generally benign and working for the good of the land, the river goddesses could become angry, flooding the surrounding countryside and carrying away whatever they wished. There is indeed a tradition on most of Ireland's waterways that a sacrifice is demanded every few years, and drowning accidents were attributed to the river goddess taking her rightful due. 'The Shannon demands a victim every seven years,' said one young Tipperary woman quite matter-of-factly.

THE *MEASCÁN MARAÍOCHT*

An old man tells a strange tale about a West Cork river. He had leased some land along its bank that had never yet been broken to plough. These flat meadows, regularly flooded in winter rains, are known as 'inch fields' and often have very rich earth, augmented from higher upstream at regular intervals. One day, this man was out working and didn't get round to his field until late in the evening. This was his tale:

It was pretty well dark when I started the tractor up and got going on the first furrow. All of a sudden, the sky was

The prehistoric passage grave of Newgrange stands on a ridge above the River Boyne.

filled with these huge wild birds. I couldn't tell whether they were geese or swans, for it was dark, but they came all around me, their wings flapping, till I couldn't see a thing for them. There must have been hundreds. I got a scare and thought I'd better get out of there, so I started to make for the gateway, but I couldn't find it! I went round and round that field, the birds still flapping and circling, and I could not find the way out. Well, I sat there and couldn't think what to do, when all of a sudden I heard the church bell ring midnight. And with that, the birds disappeared in an instant. When I looked up, I could see the gateway there, just where it always was – only it hadn't been there when I was searching for it. I've never known the like of it, and I don't want to know it again. I never went back to plough that field again, I can tell you.

This confusion and loss of sense of direction, known as the *meascán maraíocht*, is a condition usually experienced in bogland or marshy fields at night. The traveller, although he may know the place well, is suddenly unable to tell which way he should turn, where home lies, or where the gap in the bank should be. Tradition warns that if the *meascán maraíocht* does occur, you should never try to climb a wall or a ditch to get out of the area. If you do, you will find yourself a long way away next morning, with no explanation of how you got there. The inexplicable appearance of the wild birds, though, is a fascinating aspect, especially as it happened not to an inexperienced urban dweller but to a sensible elderly farmer who knew his countryside well.

But the postscript to that tale is even stranger. Months later I shared a café table with a woman in the same village. I recounted the story, regretting that I hadn't established the exact location. Her response was immediate: 'Of course. That's not a field anyone should plough. It'll be the one where all the gypsies were encamped one night half a century ago. The river rose unexpectedly in the night and swept them all away and they were drowned.'

LEGENDS OF THE LAKES

By Lough Neagh's banks where the fisherman strays
In the clear cold eve's declining,
He sees the round towers of other days
In the waves beneath him shining.

There are many legends and ancient practices around the lakes of Ireland. They are the homes of the Good People, such as Niamh of the Golden Hair, who appeared from beneath Lough Leane in Killarney to seduce Oisín away to Tir na nÓg. And beneath Lough Neagh and Lough Ree on the Shannon, fabulous underwater cities can be seen on calm evenings at sunset if you row out to the deepest part.

The custom of casting offerings into the lake waters was widespread in old Ireland, as evidenced by the rich artefacts found by archaeologists in modern times (at Lough Gur in Co Limerick, for example). Lake goddesses had to be placated and their healing powers called upon, in the same way as sacred wells.

The stories of treasure hoards in lakes
relate to genuine folk memories.

And, of course, there are often monsters lurking in the depths, charged with the guardianship of hidden treasure. One folktale tells of a lake in Co. Cavan where, one hot summer day, the topmost stones of a ruined castle became visible. One brave local lad dived down to the bottom and brought back a gold cup. But he was pursued by a giant eel who was custodian of the drowned treasure, and he barely escaped with his life.

The stories of treasure hoards in lakes relate to genuine folk memories of times of trouble when valuables were consigned to lakes for safekeeping. When the story concerns a Christian saint overcoming a fearsome monster (and there is no shortage of those), there is more to it than a fireside tale. Here it is always about the confrontation between the old ways and the new, the goddess-based nature beliefs of old Ireland versus the male-dominated new religion from Rome. In such stories, paganism is usually represented as a serpent or dragon who is vanquished by the (Christian) hero. St Patrick and the dragon of Croagh Patrick, St Finbarr and the serpent of Gougane Barra, and many more, all represent this power struggle. The undeniable fact that there have never been snakes in Ireland is conveniently set aside in the pursuit of a good Christian story!

GOUGANE SUNDAY

The tiny island of Gougane Barra is instantly recognisable as a centre of ancient power. A dark and mysterious lake is surrounded by a circle of sheltering mountains that shut out the world beyond. Importantly, it is also the source of a great river, the Lee.

Gougane has always been associated with the gift of fertility. Ancient records tell of great queens coming here to beg for the blessing of an heir, and up until it was forbidden by the Christian Church, it was not unknown for women to spend the night sleeping on the island itself for the same reason. Tellingly, one of the great ancient stones of this valley is known as the Bed of Diarmuid and Gráinne (of which there are many throughout Ireland). When the monastery was built on the island, that stone

Gougane Barra, a centre
of ancient power.

was taken and built into its walls, so that the pagan belief could be brought within the control of the church.

St Finbarr's festival day, usually called Gougane Sunday, is a good example of ancient ritual becoming incorporated into a newer tradition. Every autumn, around the equinox of 21st September, large numbers of pilgrims make their way to this valley, hidden in the mountains of Co. Cork. They come to attend a service at the chapel on the island, to make the rounds (three, seven or nine times), and say special prayers. Sedate and prayerful as it may be today, in the 19th century it was the scene of so much unbridled enjoyment that the clergy tried (and, incidentally, failed) to put a stop to the whole thing.

But that's not the only unusual thing about Gougane Sunday. Around noon, someone will shout and point up to the ridges of the surrounding hills. There, etched clearly against the sky, will be several black dots. As you gaze, more and more will appear from different points. These are the pilgrims who have started at dawn from various points in Cork and Kerry, from farmyards

Gougane Barra's lakeside chapel, waiting peacefully for the autumn gathering.

and laneways, tracks and heathery boreens. Now they are slowly descending from the hilltops, making their way through tumbled rocks, rushing streams, great masses of prickly furze, down and ever downwards, until at last men, women, children and dogs join the waiting crowds on the lakeshore with many a burst of laughter and much shaking of hands.

People have been coming over the hills to Gougane on this day for hundreds of years. Some are simply following the old Mass roads to the church here, and that is one part of the story, but the tradition goes back further still.

The official Christian legend of Gougane Barra is that St Finbarr, seeking a remote hermitage, found his way to this lake and set up his simple cell on the island, driving out the resident (and clearly pagan) serpent. Stray and tantalisingly vague references in ancient Irish documents, however, seem to suggest that as a child Finbarr was, in fact, sent to study at the lake island. Given the time frame, could this have been a druidic school? Like St Columba, was the much-loved St Finbarr originally a keeper of ancient druidic wisdom who converted to Christianity? Or did the Christian Church, recognising the power of Gougane, create its own legend to bring the sacred place under its wing?

Some say that the Serpent of Gougane is still to be seen surfacing in the lake from time to time.

'Nonsense,' says Breda Lucey robustly. 'I've lived here all my life and I've never seen it.'

Son Neil, who runs the Gougane Barra hotel, isn't so sure. 'You'd glimpse strange things on that lake at dusk now and again.'

Thin Places & Thorn Trees

In Ireland the Otherworld is always near at hand, over your shoulder, down the lane. There are special places embedded all over the landscape – special in ancient times, and special now. They are often known as 'thin places', for it is here, where the veil between worlds is transparent, that you come closest to encountering the Wise Ones.

FAIRY FORTS

The ancient earthen enclosures known as fairy forts, or raths, are to be seen everywhere in Ireland, and no-one would think of building here or damaging them in any way. This prohibition extends too to fairy paths – the routes that the Good People are believed to take when they travel between their underground palaces at certain times of the year, notably Bealtaine and Samhain.

Lady Carbery of Castlefreke had no idea she was contravening an ancient belief when she had a pretty little stone cottage built in the woods at Rathbarry in the 19th century to house a sprigging school – a place where local girls could learn to make lace and thus supplement their family income. When the school fell into disuse, she offered it to a local man who had no home of his own, expecting him to be delighted. Much embarrassed, he refused the gift. It was only after much pressure on Lady Carbery's part that he explained. She had had the cottage built right across a fairy path and bad luck would surely come to anyone who dared to live there. The Sprigging School is still there today, and is a popular motif for tourist cameras. Nobody stays there overnight though.

FAIRY WIND AND HUNGRY GRASS

The next time you see a little whirlwind of dry leaves suddenly rising from the ground and circling before blowing away, be sure to bow or raise your hat. It's caused by a fairy wind, and it means the Good People are passing.

And it is always a good idea to keep a crust of bread in your pocket if you are walking alone in the hills. Should a sudden desperate faintness come upon you, you'll need that sustenance, and quickly. It means you've walked on the Hungry Grass – a spot where some poor soul died of starvation in centuries past. This is another example of the melding of myth and historical fact,

The Rathbarry Sprigging School – a place where local girls could learn to make lace.

since the many pitiful famine graveyards in the countryside are a reminder that there was a time when hunger hovered over many homes, and lurked around every corner.

CURSING STONES

A peculiar custom that still survives in several parts of the country is the use of cursing stones – although it might be more positive to regard them as wishing stones. St Brigid's Stone at Killinagh in Cavan surely must be the latter, or else the revered goddess-turned-saint must have had an unexpectedly malevolent side to her character.

In the middle of a field stands the ruin of a tiny church. Behind this is an old graveyard. In the far wall of the graveyard a section has been hollowed out over the years, showing where uncounted numbers have climbed over into the field beyond. Here, on the edge of a lake, stands the large, drum-shaped rock with several hollows in its surface. Each of these contains a smooth, rounded stone. To wish someone well, or indeed make a wish for yourself, the stone is turned sunwise. To bring ill luck on someone, it is turned against the sun, or 'widdershins'. A quaint old custom, no longer practised? Look underneath those cursing stones and you will find very modern coins, their brightness proclaiming that they haven't been there very long. There

Central cursing stone, Bonane, near Kenmare, Co. Kerry.

are similar stones in the Bonane valley near Kenmare, again sited just outside the old churchyard.

It is the ill-famed cursing stone on Tory Island off Donegal that has gathered the strongest legends. The most famous concerns the mysterious wreck of a gunboat that was headed for Tory in 1884 with bailiffs and constabulary aboard, to evict those who could not pay their rent. It was said that when the boat was glimpsed at sea, the cursing stone was deliberately turned. The ship struck the rocks and sank with the loss of fifty lives.

Cursing or wishing stones may well have been part of early druidic rituals, turned in one direction to channel positive power, and in the other to reverse the natural path and release negative force against their enemies. Although they are clearly still in use today, it is never a good idea to wish bad luck on another person. Such ill-intentioned wishes have a way of coming back on the creator. If you happen upon one of these strange ancient sites, then turn the rounded stones gently in a sunwise direction and wish well to all the world.

THE THORN TREE

If a single image could represent ancient beliefs in Ireland today, it would be the thorn tree. Often spoken of as 'the fairy tree', it is regarded with respect, if not fear. A lone thorn tree, standing proudly in a flat, ploughed field or smooth pasture, is evidence that the farmer does not dare to disturb it. Many are the tales and records of disasters following upon those who ventured to dig one up. If the thorn tree happens also to be growing on a rath, or fairy fort, then to interfere with it is unthinkable.

While many of the ancient woodlands of Ireland disappeared, the thorn tree escaped largely unscathed.

'I tell you what, I wouldn't touch that tree for anything,' says elderly farmer Daithi O'Riordan. Standing by the gate, he regards the bramble-covered mound in his field, the twisted thorn in full bloom atop its ancient stones. 'No matter what I'd need the field for, that tree stays as it is. 'Twould be asking for trouble to disturb it.'

Indeed, while many of the ancient woodlands of Ireland fell victim over centuries to the demands of humans and industry, the thorn tree escaped unscathed, due to the folk belief that it should not be touched. Damage this tree at your peril, unless it's May Day, when branches may be cut and used to protect home and farmyard for the year ahead. Just don't try it any other day of the year.

Any tree that arrives by itself is considered to be under Their protection.

We're not talking here about the numerous planted hawthorn hedges that pattern the countryside with clouds of white blossom in early summer, but of the individual, independent, lone trees that have chosen to root themselves in unexpected spots, giving no explanation and asking for no assistance. Any tree that arrives by itself is considered to be under Their protection, and the hawthorn doubly so. It may mark an entrance to the Otherworld, or be the actual home of one of the Good People, many of whom enjoy dwelling in among its green leaves and fragrant flowers. When you come across a sacred well, often the tree that bends protectively over it is a hawthorn, its spiny branches carrying an assortment of rags and other offerings tied on by visitors in search of help.

There is also the deep-rooted belief, still held in many country areas, that the twisted lone thorn tree glimpsed atop a windswept rock may be one of the Good People in disguise, keeping watch over the land. Sometimes it is even the Cailleach, or Wise Old One, who now and again takes the form of a weary old traveller and moves among the people for a while.

The twisted lone thorn tree glimpsed atop a windswept rock may be one of the Good People in disguise.

'She saw a queer black shadow on the ground, like a bent old woman with a basket and a stick, running before the wind. She looked up, and there was the twisted tree on the high rock. It was exactly like the old woman who had gone the roads with her.'

From *King of the Tinkers* by Patricia Lynch

That traditional song, 'The Fairy Tree', made famous by Count John McCormack, demonstrates the fascinating mixture of legend, tradition, history and religious influence that makes Irish folklore such a complex maze. Isabel Leslie is credited with writing the lyrics, but it is possible that she took an older version and interpolated the Christian verse to render it more acceptable. Thus the song is a prime example of how the old religion and the new, together with historic events, became blended in the public perception.

The Fairy Tree

All night around the thorn tree, the little people play,
And men and women passing will turn their heads away.
But if your heart's a child's heart and if your eyes are clean,
You'll never fear the thorn tree that grows beyond Clogheen.

They'll tell you dead men hung there, its black and bitter fruit,
To guard the buried treasure round which it twines its root.
They'll tell you Cromwell hung them, but that could never be,
He'd be in dread like others to touch the Fairy Tree.

But Katie Ryan who saw there in some sweet dream she had,
The Blessed Son of Mary and all his face was sad.
She dreamt she heard him say, 'Why should they be afraid,
When, from a branch of thorn tree, the crown I wore was made?'

By moonlight round the thorn tree, the little people play
And men and women passing will turn their heads away.
But if your heart's a child's heart and if your eyes are clean,
You'll never fear the thorn tree that grows beyond Clogheen.

[Lyrics: Isabel Leslie, 1930]

Magical Birds & Beasts

*I*n the Celtic world, nothing is quite what it seems, and nothing can be taken for granted, not even the cat purring around your feet or the wren scolding from a nearby bush. Familiar though they may be, it behoves us to treat them with respect and caution.

CATS

In Ireland, while the cat's useful work around house and barn in keeping mice and rats at bay is well appreciated, it is still regarded with some suspicion. When they leap out of a window at night and don't return until morning, it is likely that they are roistering with the Good Folk or even visiting the Cat Sidhe in his mountain fort. The Cat Sidhe, or Fairy Cat, is an Otherworld creature who appears as a large black feline with one white spot on his breast. He tends to turn up if you're wandering somewhere you shouldn't be – by a fairy fort after dark, for example, or on one of Their pathways that should not be trodden by humans – and his arched back and blazing green eyes will leave you in no doubt of your error. From this creature springs the belief that it is bad luck to have any black cat cross your path. However, if a black cat should choose your house to live in (and it is they who make the choice, not you), treat it with all courtesy and kindness, and good luck will be with the household. If you do not, woe betide!

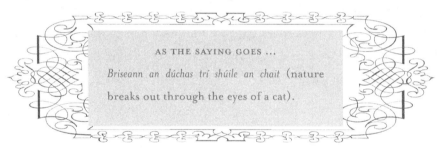

AS THE SAYING GOES …

Briseann an dúchas trí shúile an chait (nature breaks out through the eyes of a cat).

DOGS

Dogs tend to be faithful to their human companions and not given to wandering, never really happy away from their owner's side. They also have special qualities: Not only does a dog know that a storm is on the way at least half an hour before you see signs in the skies, it can also, unerringly, sniff out an enchanted being in the vicinity, even if disguised.

If your dog therefore gives chase to a hare crossing your fields on a May morning, it's trying to get it off your land as soon as

Wise women, particularly those of malevolent nature, are known to change themselves into hares.

possible. Wise women, particularly those of malevolent nature, are known to change themselves into hares in order to travel around without being noticed, or even to work spells on those against whom they have a grudge. May morning is a particularly dangerous time for this, as the dew is especially powerful then, and the disguised hare can work havoc by circling and sweeping the dewdrops from the wet grass. Many are the stories of hares being shot with a silver sixpence (ordinary bullets will not do), and an old woman subsequently being discovered in her cottage, badly wounded.

The dog always knows when bad weather is coming. Half an hour before a storm hits, it's in, scratching and whining at the door. And if the cat has its back to the fire, that's a sure sign of rain.

SHAPE SHIFTERS

Like the gods of ancient Greece, the Good People will often don disguises or shape-change when visiting the human world. That most feared goddess of war and death, the Mórrígan, habitually assumed the silky-black plumage, cruel beak and treacherous talons of a raven, the better to soar over battlefields or appear warningly in front of troops marching to conflict. As we have seen, the raven was also used by druids for foretelling future events, and the folk memory of this survives in an implicit belief of the raven's cunning. Country folk today still fear and mistrust this large black bird with its echoing croak, and that mistrust has been further extended to rooks and crows – even to the magpie, which is a relatively recent immigrant, only having arrived in Ireland in the 19th century.

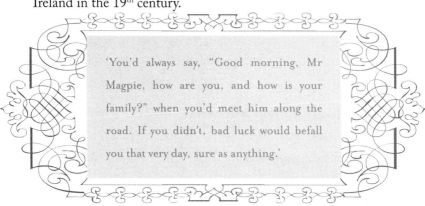

'You'd always say, "Good morning, Mr Magpie, how are you, and how is your family?" when you'd meet him along the road. If you didn't, bad luck would befall you that very day, sure as anything.'

The goddess Boann, deity of the river Boyne, on the other hand, is kindly, and can appear in the guise of a white cow bringing fertility and good fortune to your land. From time to time, a local farmer could also be blessed by the unexpected appearance of strange cows in his fields, often seeming to come from the nearby river or lake. Otherworld cows, believed to be sent by Boann, are always white with red ears, and although they will bring great fortune, they must be treated with respect. Otherwise they will return to the river, taking all their offspring with them (and your luck too). Sea horses, born of the foam-tipped waves, may also come to shore and breed superb stock, but they can disappear again just as magically. And Ireland is, of course, famous for its horses; many Irish winners of international races have given rise to whispers that there is surely fairy blood in their veins.

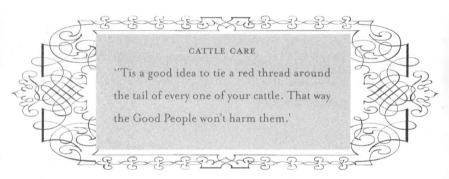

CATTLE CARE

'Tis a good idea to tie a red thread around the tail of every one of your cattle. That way the Good People won't harm them.'

SEALS

Seals, on the other hand, are true Otherworld beings who assume their sleek, sea-rounded shape by choice. There are many tales of beautiful seal women being captured by enterprising young men who marry them and raise large families. The way to do this is to discover one asleep in some secret cove, when her seal skin will be shed temporarily. If you are lucky enough to come upon one of these beings, and take and hide her seal skin, she is yours; but should she ever discover where you have hidden it, she will return once more to the world beneath the sea and leave you heartbroken. The singing of the seal women – kin to the mermaids and sirens of other countries – is very beautiful, like the music of the Otherworld itself. And this you can actually hear for yourself. All it takes is a sheltered spot above a remote cliff, and some patience. The Saltee Islands off Wexford are often a concert hall for the strange echoing song of the seals lying on seaweed-strewn rocky couches far below. Like the calling of the whales, it's a sound that stays with you forever.

TELLING THE BEES

Bees must always be informed when someone is born, visits or dies in your house. The accepted method is to go out late in the evening, knock softly on the hive, bow or curtsey, and tell them the news. Until recently it was a custom to tie bands of black crepe around beehives when a death occurred in the family. If the bees are not told, they may leave your hives, taking prosperity with them.

FOXES

Foxes (along with cats and red-haired women) are perceived as bad luck if met on the road first thing in the morning, but they are also honoured for their cunning. It is believed that a fox will often lie down and pretend to be dead, so as to lure unwary geese

Foxes (along with cats and red-haired women) may be perceived as bad luck.

or hens to their fate. Many have claimed to see foxes ridding their fur of fleas by backing slowly into a river with a tuft of moss held between their front paws. As the water creeps higher, the fleas decamp to the moss, which is then loosed by the fox and left to float downriver.

A very curious and well-attested tradition was still being observed at Gormanstown Castle in Co. Meath up to the mid-20th century. Whenever the head of the family was near death, foxes would quietly and slowly begin to assemble from the surrounding woods into a vast circle around the castle. Here they stayed until life had departed. Hen coops were safe during this vigil, nor would the castle's guard dogs attack them. The castle, however, was sold to the Franciscans in the late 1940s, and the foxes clearly felt their family obligation to be at an end – there is no record of their appearance since.

Creatures of the Shadows

*N*ot all Otherworld creatures are beautiful women with melodious voices. Legends and old texts alike tell us that the lakes and rivers of Ireland are full of strange and threatening beasts, or *péists*, who seize and drown anyone unwise enough to challenge them. Ditto are particular mountains, caves and valleys. Poulnapeasta in Co. Clare, Altnapaste in Donegal, Cornapeast in Monaghan, all enshrine the frightening memory of some horror. Knocknapeasta in MacGillycuddy's Reeks in Kerry looks down over Lough Cummeenpeasta, a double deterrent to hillwalkers. Carrigaphooca Castle in Co. Cork enshrines the memory of the fairy rock on which it is built.

Carrigaphooca Castle is built on the 'rock of the pooka'.

Monsters are also associated with ruined castles and fairy forts, where they lurk in hiding, ready to attack anyone disturbing their peace. Fionn Mac Cumhaill is credited with disposing of many fearsome creatures:

> *He slew the spectre of Drom Cliabh,*
> *And the spectre and serpent of Lough Ree.*
> *Fionn banished from the raths*
> *Each peist he went to meet.*
> *A serpent in the refulgent Shannon*
> *He slew by frequenting the lake.*
>
> (*Transactions of the Ossianic Society*)

188

LAKESIDE FIENDS

In Lake Gurteen near Bunratty Castle, a monstrous pike is said to emerge and crawl up the banks at night to seize lambs and calves. Unsurprisingly, swimming is not popular there.

In Kilmacreehy Church on the shores of Liscannor Bay in Co. Clare is a strange carving on the tomb of one MacCreehy. Its long, pointed ears, large eyes and huge jaws bristling with pointed teeth make it a frightening monster, and one wonders what inspired the original sculptor. Locals have called it a dragon for centuries.

There are similar carvings on Scattery Island in the Shannon estuary, where a monstrous creature called Cathach terrorised inhabitants until St Senan arrived to expel it. (The old Irish name for Scattery is Inis Cathaigh.)

Lough Allen, also on the Shannon, is guarded by Aiollfhion, who is capable of raising a storm in minutes if aggrieved. She has been seen from time to time, a monstrous creature with a massive head and serpentine body.

The monster at Lough Ree (yes, that's on the Shannon too; our mightiest river would appear to have more than its fair share of protective creatures), although officially recorded on Fionn Mac Cumhaill's fiend-slaying checklist, must have had nine lives because he continues to crop up in the records through the ages. In the 7th century, St Mochua of Balla told of a pursued stag who swam to safety on an island in Lough Ree, where none dared to follow for fear of the monster. One hunter did at last make the attempt, but was, predictably, devoured.

Over the centuries, sightings of the Lough Ree fiend have continued. The creature's appearance as recently as 1960 created a national sensation, since he was seen by three priests, presumably impeccable witnesses.

> *It was moving. It went down under the water and came up again in the form of a loop. The length from the end of the coil to the head was six feet. There was about eighteen inches of head and neck over the water. The head and neck were narrow in comparison to the thickness of a good-sized salmon. It was getting its propulsion from underneath the water, and we did not see all of it.*
>
> (*Westmeath Independent*, 28th May 1960)

Fergus Mac Leide of Ulster is remembered for tackling the fearsome female monster Muirdris at Lough Rudraige in Co. Down. For this, he made good use of a pair of magical shoes gifted to him by Iubdan the leprechaun, which enabled the wearer to travel freely underwater.

> *Fergus said to the men of Ulster: 'Bide here and sit you all down, that ye may witness how I and the monster shall deal together.' Then he, being shod with Iubdan's shoes, leapt into the loch, erect and brilliant and brave, making for the monster. At sound of the hero's approach, she bared her teeth as does a wolf-dog threatened with a club; her eyes blazed like two great torches kindled, suddenly she put forth her sharp claws' jagged array, bent her neck with the curve of an arch and clenched her glittering tusks, throwing back her ears hideously, till her whole semblance was one of gloomy cruel*

fury. Alas, for any in this world that should be fated to do battle with that monster: huge-headed, long-fanged dragon that she was! The fearsome and colossal creature's form was this: a crest and mane she had of coarse hair, a mouth that yawned, deep-sunken eyes; on either side thrice fifty flippers, each armed with as many claws recurved; a body impregnable. Thrice fifty feet her extended altitude; round as an apple she was in contraction, but in bulk equalled some great hill in its rough garb of furze.

A fearsome dog-creature known as the *Dobhar-chú,* or water hound, is depicted on a 17th-century gravestone in Co. Leitrim, where it is said to have killed an unfortunate woman who was washing clothes in Glenade Lough. But that wasn't the last heard of it: it has also been seen as recently as 2003 on a lake in Connemara.

THE POOKA

The Pooka, or *Púca,* is a well-known creature of Irish legend, familiar to every man, woman and child in Ireland today. In shape a great black horse with fiery eyes, he is definitely not of this world, but neither is he a god in disguise. The Pooka is a free spirit, more given to making mischief than dealing injury or

The Pooka is a free spirit, more given to making mischief than dealing injury or death.

death, and as such there tends to be a sort of affection for him, in the way that one is exasperatedly fond of a recalcitrant pet.

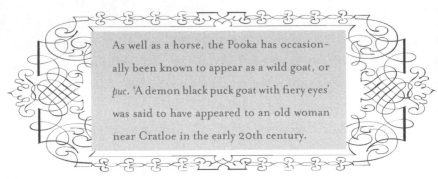

As well as a horse, the Pooka has occasionally been known to appear as a wild goat, or *puc*. 'A demon black puck goat with fiery eyes' was said to have appeared to an old woman near Cratloe in the early 20th century.

The Pooka's favourite trick is to rise up suddenly underneath some innocent fellow rambling home at midnight from the pub. Throwing his victim across his broad back, he will take him on a wild ride across the hills and mountains, only tumbling him off into a muddy bog as dawn approaches. The poor man then not only has to undertake the long journey home, but also to explain what happened him when he gets there.

There are innumerable place names dedicated to this rapscallion all over the country, from Poulaphouca (cave of the pooka), and Bóthar na bPúca (road of the pooka) to Carrigaphooca (rock of the pooka). The little village of Beaufort near Killarney has a far more interesting name in the original Irish: Lios na bPúca, or fairy fort of the pooka.

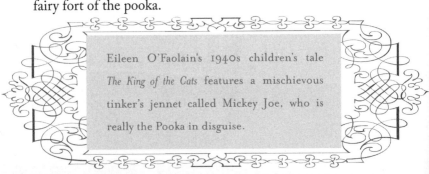

Eileen O'Faolain's 1940s children's tale *The King of the Cats* features a mischievous tinker's jennet called Mickey Joe, who is really the Pooka in disguise.

The Little Shoemaker

The leprechaun is probably the most familiar image of Ireland. Sometimes called the *cluricaun*, this master shoemaker to the *sidhe* and guardian of buried treasure is most often seen sitting underneath the fairy thorn or maybe a furze bush bright with yellow, coconut-scented blossom. He taps away with his tiny gold hammer on miniature slippers of silk and satin, or doll-sized hunting boots of soft green leather. His famed crock of gold may be close by – or safely buried at the foot of the rainbow that arches over the valley.

The Irish landscape is full
of secret corners, fit for
a leprechaun's gold.

Unlike the rest of the Good People, who enjoy nothing more than gathering together to sing, dance and enjoy music, the leprechaun is a solitary fellow, preferring his own company. He can be quite bad-tempered if you surprise him, but he can switch instantly to charm, the better to distract you and make his escape.

The most important thing to remember if you catch a leprechaun is that you never let go of him, and never take your eyes off him for one instant. If you do, he'll be gone in a flash. Many are the sad stories of those lucky enough to capture the canny shoemaker, only to be tricked into losing him again.

One of the best-known tales concerns a wily farmer who caught a leprechaun and wouldn't let him go. When the farmer insisted on being shown where the crock of gold was buried, the leprechaun took him to a field. In the middle was growing one plant of *buachalán buidhe* (yellow ragwort).

'Wait a minute, so,' said the farmer, pulling off one of his bright green garters and fastening it around the plant. 'Now be off with you!'

The leprechaun needed no further encouragement and was off behind the nearest hedge in a twinkling. The farmer ran hastily home to get a spade and came back again, whistling as he thought of the riches almost within his grasp. When he got to the field, though, he stopped short in shock and fury. Wasn't it now full of brilliant golden *buachalán buidhe* – and every one of them with an identical green garter around it!

Where did he come from, what are the origins of this little man in his green coat and tall hat, with such a skill for working with leather and gold nails? The old tale of King Fergus Mac Leide

In one story, a *buachalán buidhe* (yellow ragwort) helped the leprechaun hide his gold.

gives us a clue. It tells of the far-away kingdom of Faylinn, where the Wee Folk or leprechauns live. Their king, Iubdan, decides to visit 'the land of giants'. King Fergus is so delighted with his unexpected little guest, he is unwilling to let him return home. At last Iubdan buys his freedom with a pair of magical shoes made in white bronze that enable their wearer to travel underwater with perfect ease. These are used by Fergus to vanquish a monster – but he is himself dealt a death blow in the process. You can never trust the gift of a leprechaun. It will always come back at you some way.

It is probably those magical shoes that gave the leprechaun his reputation of being a fine cobbler. The legend of his crock of gold stems from an earlier belief that he is the guardian of a great treasure hoard, buried in troubled times past. Indeed the occasional discovery, whether by accident or archaeology, of some superb piece of gold or silvercraft long buried in Irish soil does give grounds for believing in such hoards. This protective role links him to the trolls and dwarves of Norse regions who also mount guard over unimaginable riches. Perhaps the leprechaun is waiting for the rightful owner to return and claim his own. Don't try to pull the wool over his eyes, though. He will know if you're not the right one.

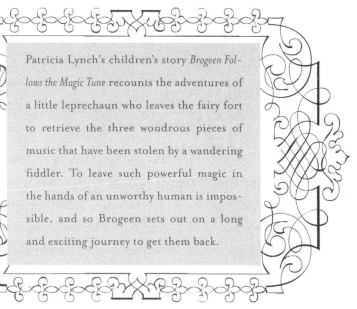

Patricia Lynch's children's story *Brogeen Follows the Magic Tune* recounts the adventures of a little leprechaun who leaves the fairy fort to retrieve the three wondrous pieces of music that have been stolen by a wandering fiddler. To leave such powerful magic in the hands of an unworthy human is impossible, and so Brogeen sets out on a long and exciting journey to get them back.

Seasonal Merry-Making

As well as special places in the landscape, in Ireland there are also special times of the year, when the veil that hides the Otherworld from us becomes almost transparent. It is then that the Good People are more likely to come visiting, and unwary humans may be drawn across into Tír na nÓg.

This happens at those natural divisions of the year, when the spirits controlling wind and rain, sunshine and storm, fertility and growth, must be invoked and honoured. The Celtic calendar intersects the four great lunar festivals with the two solar festivals of midwinter and midsummer.

If you want to keep close to the ancient calendar today, then go outside and look to the shape of the moon.

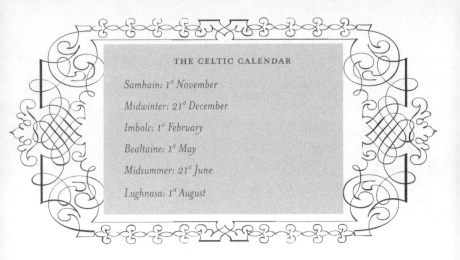

THE CELTIC CALENDAR

Samhain: 1ˢᵗ November

Midwinter: 21ˢᵗ December

Imbolc: 1ˢᵗ February

Bealtaine: 1ˢᵗ May

Midsummer: 21ˢᵗ June

Lughnasa: 1ˢᵗ August

The dates were not precisely fixed in ancient times but would have been calculated on the phases of the moon and sun by druids, who were skilled in observing the skies. The druids then informed the king or local leader of the date on which the ceremonies should begin. The lunar festivals would centre on the night of the full moon, and the solar observances when the sun was at its highest or lowest point in the yearly cycle; celebrations would take place up to two or three days on either side.

The six festivals of the ancient Celtic world were times of magic and merry-making.

Untamed Moon: Lunar Feasts

*I*f you want to keep close to the ancient calendar, then go outside and look to the shape of the moon or observe the lengthening or shortening days rather than relying on a wall calendar. Good gardeners do this anyway, since not only is daylight essential for growth, but many plants do better if planted under a waxing moon, while others prefer a waning crescent. Nature follows the guidance of the skies, and we should too.

SAMHAIN: CELTIC NEW YEAR

The Celtic year begins at Samhain, summer's end. The onset of the dark months might seem more like a time of winding down instead of beginning, an end rather than a start, but the Celtic philosophy is that growth starts slowly beneath the ground, so that when the sun returns, everything will be ready to burst forth. That is another bit of good gardening practice today: to plant seeds in the autumn, before the warmth has quite left the earth. In this way they are far more likely to do well in the spring than seeds thrust suddenly into unwelcoming soil still holding the chill of winter.

Hazelnuts and apples were harvested and stored away as vital winter food in an age long before the potato reached Ireland. They meant more than food, though. The apple has always been regarded in Celtic myth and legend as a symbol of fertility, its delicate blossom in late spring promising rich fruit in the autumn. It's a fruit of Tír na nÓg, the Land of Youth, and the Good People often carry a branch of golden apples as evidence of the delights to be found in their own country. What hero could resist the temptation of such an apple, offered by a beautiful woman who beckons him to follow her to a more glorious world? It is an image which the Christian Church was later to twist for its own purposes in the tale of the Garden of Eden.

TRADITIONAL GAMES

Sunset comes early on 31st October, and excitement in many family farmhouses is reaching fever point. There is a great galvanised washtub full of water on the floor, with rosy apples bobbing up and down in it. From the rafters hang more apples on long strings, coming just down to the level of a young face. In the place of honour on the table is the fortune-telling barm brack (*báirín breac*, or speckled fruit loaf). A basket of hazelnuts sits in the hearth by the turf fire. In the window, left uncurtained this night, a turnip is roughly carved into the shape of a hideous face. The stub of candle placed inside makes the demonic eyes flicker.

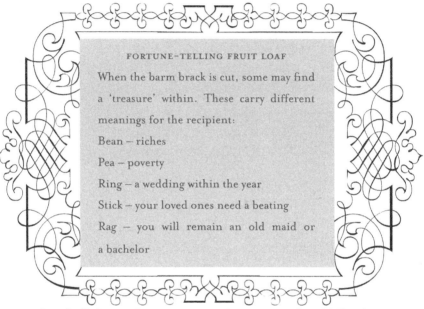

FORTUNE-TELLING FRUIT LOAF

When the barm brack is cut, some may find a 'treasure' within. These carry different meanings for the recipient:

Bean – riches

Pea – poverty

Ring – a wedding within the year

Stick – your loved ones need a beating

Rag – you will remain an old maid or a bachelor

Amid all the modern commercial trappings, the old Samhain customs are as enthusiastically observed as ever. Apple bobbing and the other traditions may be children's games now, but they descend from ancient rituals practised by the adults of a community. It was adults who tried to seize the apple as it swung from the rafters or bobbed in the tub of water, thereby grasping the promise of fertility for themselves, their families, their flocks and their fields. They would crack the ripe hazelnuts and toss the shells onto the fire, or lay the unshelled nuts in the embers to see if they leapt in one direction or another.

Apple bobbing and the other traditions may be children's games now, but they descend from ancient rituals.

Even the popular 'trick or treating', in which children dress up as evil creatures and go from house to house in search of reward, comes from ritual observances. At Samhain, there are many spirits about, both mild and malevolent. Those who have crossed over into the Otherworld during the year choose this time to revisit their former dwellings to see that their memory is being honoured and their lands cared for. Families will put out food and leave the door ajar, to show these visitors are welcome.

Others are not so welcome. There is mischief about at Samhain too. In ancient Ireland, no-one would go out on this night unless forced so to do. Members of a clan would travel long distances to foregather with their fellows at the court of their king and celebrate the festival with much merry-making, while the court druids lit bonfires and performed rituals to keep evil from their midst.

Going from house to house in ghostly robes is fun for children today, but the custom arose from a need to protect home and hearth. If malevolent spirits approached a settlement, they would believe that others of their kind were there before them, and so would head off somewhere else. The children at your door at Halloween are doing you signal service by warning off something more unpleasant, and they deserve little gifts as reward for their labours!

HALLOWEEN HAZEL

The central myth of the Celtic world concerns the nine hazel trees of wisdom that grew around the magical spring at the source of the River Boyne, their nuts being eaten by the Salmon of Knowledge as they dropped into the water. Ceremonially eating the kernels while at the same time observing how the shells behave when thrown on the fire, is another form of fortune-telling, linked to a wish for wisdom and enlightenment.

THE MONSTER OF TARA

It was at the feast of Samhain that Fionn Mac Cumhaill first approached the High King at Tara to offer his services as a warrior. The king revealed that his court had been troubled for many years with the visit of a dreadful monster called Aillen. The monster would first lull everyone to sleep with magical music, and then set the castle on fire. Of course Fionn managed to outwit and kill the monster, thereby securing his future both at Tara and as head of the legendary Fianna. Anyone who could withstand the forces of evil at this most dangerous time of the year was worth holding on to.

Bonfires and indeed fireworks are also relics of ancient rituals against bad luck and evil spirits. Fire drove such negative energies away, especially when built of magical woods, and explosions had a similar effect. While bonfires can be seen all over Ireland at Samhain, in England many of the rituals have been transferred to 5th November, Guy Fawkes Night. In the normal course of events, one man's failed attempt to blow up the Houses of Parliament would hardly warrant a strongly observed annual celebration, but it suited England well to distance itself from a festival that had already, by that time, been taken over by the Catholic Church and rechristened All Hallows Eve – or Halloween for short.

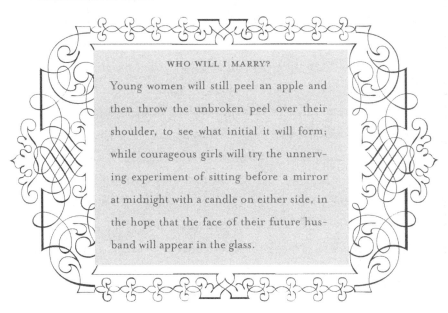

WHO WILL I MARRY?

Young women will still peel an apple and then throw the unbroken peel over their shoulder, to see what initial it will form; while courageous girls will try the unnerving experiment of sitting before a mirror at midnight with a candle on either side, in the hope that the face of their future husband will appear in the glass.

Bonfires and indeed fireworks are relics of ancient rituals against bad luck and evil spirits.

IMBOLC: HERALD OF SPRING

It's the first day of February and a damp, drizzly morning in the heart of Killarney National Park. That hasn't deterred anyone, though. The Biddy Dancers have arrived and where they are, the crowds will follow. The men and women of the group are adjusting their white costumes, carefully putting on their intricately plaited straw hats. The music strikes up, and the dancers march to a lively tune towards the gardens of stately Muckross House, led by the man chosen to carry the Brídóg, a wooden figure dressed in white with a coronet of green ribbons. These effigies stretch back to earliest Celtic Ireland to honour Brigit, who cared for humans, animals and the land, and beg her to break the grip of winter.

In ancient times, Biddy Dancers would go from house to house, setting up the Brídóg in a place of honour, dancing in the kitchens, receiving a warm welcome everywhere. Today they follow the same custom, gathering in public houses and hotels to let everyone know that Imbolc is here. The Beaufort Biddies have been dancing in the pubs around Kerry for the past week or so, but today, the feast of Brigit itself, they come to do her honour in the open air amid the trees and fields, as befits a spring festival. A little wooden platform has already been set up for them and soon feet are flying in a traditional set dance. The crowds clap and laugh, and eventually start dancing too.

Looking at this veneration of the goddess Brigit, it is not hard to see where the tradition of carrying a statue of the Blessed Virgin through the streets on festive days originated. But this goddess has become reclothed for many in the garb of the Christian St Brigid, whose feast day is celebrated on 1st February.

Much of the symbolism associated with the goddess Brigit has undoubtedly been lost, yet much is still observed. Fifty years ago, children would make their own little Brídógs out of straw and carry them from house to house, asking for sweets or pennies. Similarly the children would be encouraged to collect evergreens, ferns and colourful fabric to decorate the local sacred well, usually dedicated to St Brigid.

Today, the making of Brigid's Cross is widely practised. In the weeks coming up to Imbolc, schoolchildren are taught the skill in the classroom, while workshops are arranged in clubs for adults who might have forgotten how to do it or missed the experience in childhood. Different parts of the country have different shapes of cross, some large and elaborate, some simple.

The older of the two St Brigid's wells in Kildare town.

There is even a special three-legged cross to put in cowsheds and stables. It wouldn't do at all to have the wrong kind of cross in the wrong place!

In a local library, one old man holds up his rush cross with a satisfied air. 'There now, that's the first one I've made in many years, but I haven't lost the knack. I'll bring it home and hang it over the door. That's what we did when I was young.'

A young housewife nods. 'I remember going out below our house and pulling the rushes from the boggy ground. You have to pull them for Brigid's Cross, not cut them.'

The making of Brigid's Cross is as widely practised today as it ever was.

BEALTAINE: CELEBRATION OF FERTILITY

You could get lost in these winding country boreens, especially now with all the lush growth of early summer giving every bit of stone wall or earth bank another foot or two of grass and wild flowers. Dog roses trail in decorative arches, brushing against the car with a shower of pink petals as you look out for a signpost to the Cathair.

At last, there it is. Across a bridge, up a hill and suddenly a venerable stone wall at the very top, enclosing a large, circular grassy area with a magnificent view over the border lands of Cork and Kerry.

Battered farm vehicles, many with trailers and boxes, are parked everywhere, for this is May Day, Bealtaine, the first day of summer. As in earlier times, when cattle were driven into the hills to graze for the season – a practice known throughout Europe as transhumance, and in Ireland called 'booleying', from *buaile*, to travel – so now animals are brought here to a sacred well reserved especially for them. For centuries, people have led their sheep and goats, horses and cattle, to drink at this source on May morning, while others come to fill a bottle, which is stored in barn or byre and used throughout the year to treat animal ailments.

'We'd be looking forward to it for months,' affirms one elderly man, stowing his bottle of water carefully away in a capacious pocket. 'It was the biggest time of the year for us, and the start of summer made it a great day out.'

Entire families would gather at the Cathair from late on May Eve to eat and drink and celebrate with their friends. So popular did it continue to be that local clergy denounced both the place and the event from the pulpit. It didn't stop people from coming though.

What cannot be changed must be controlled, and the signs of church influence are visible at the Cathair today. A small plaster statue of the Virgin Mary stands on the western wall, surrounded by a number of flat stones that have been inscribed many times over with rough crosses. On the weekend nearest to May Day, people assemble to circle the old fortification sunwise, say a specific number of prayers, and take their turn at incising yet again the old outlines on the stones with a sharp pebble.

The real purpose of the site is evident, however, when you turn your back on the makeshift altar and face east, towards the great grey stone which stands in the centre of the enclosure. Towering above it, clearly outlined against the sky some miles away, are the twin mounds of the Paps of Danu, ancient sites of worship of the great Earth Mother. This, then, is one of the earliest places of gathering for ritual worship at Bealtaine, saluting the sun as it rose between the Paps and carrying out the observances that hopefully would ensure a prosperous summer. Cows given the blessing of the sacred water would undoubtedly do well and produce much milk for butter and cheese during their summer booleying in the hills, while their calves would grow strong and healthy. And Danu would smile on her people for gathering to honour her on this day.

CEREMONIAL FIRE

Druids would light bonfires on May morning to honour the nature gods. All household fires were extinguished the evening before and only lit again with a brand from this ceremonial blaze. In the 20th century, cattle were driven through the bonfire smoke to give them additional good health. Today the Bealtaine bonfire has largely been transferred to the midsummer festivals.

THE DEW OF THE FIELDS

Bealtaine is one of the two most ancient and powerful festivals in the Celtic calendar (the other being Samhain) and carries innumerable beliefs, customs, traditions, warnings and dangers. The Good People go travelling at this time, of course, but so do those of evil intent, as it is easier to carry out wicked deeds when normal barriers are down.

Even the simplest natural occurrence is fraught with danger. The very dew on your fields is highly potent at dawn on May Day; young women still go out early to bathe their faces in its crystal drops, thereby ensuring lifelong beauty. However, that same dew and the plants on which it falls must be guarded, because someone could cast a spell on it to draw away your luck in churning butter, in getting milk from your cows, even in the health of your grass.

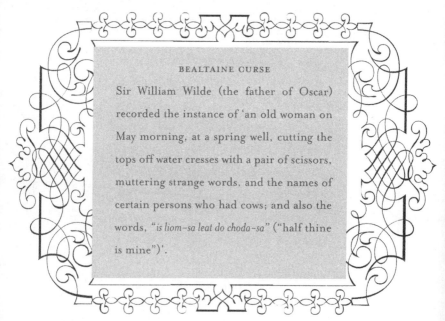

BEALTAINE CURSE

Sir William Wilde (the father of Oscar) recorded the instance of 'an old woman on May morning, at a spring well, cutting the tops off water cresses with a pair of scissors, muttering strange words, and the names of certain persons who had cows; and also the words, *"is liom-sa leat do choda-sa"* ("half thine is mine")'.

It was also considered unwise to give away either fire or water on May Day, even if a neighbour begged a light for her fire, or a simple drink. To do so would endanger your household for the entire year. Children could be at risk too. One Kerry woman remembered that when she was a child in the 1920s, her mother used to mark a cross on their petticoats on May Eve with a burnt stick, to protect them from the fairies. In Donegal, a mother who had to leave her babe unattended even for a moment on this day of all days would lay a piece of iron – the poker would do – across the cradle so that the child would not be snatched by the Good People.

The best-loved tradition was to bring home the May blossom – the white flowers of hawthorn that are abundant at this time of year. This is the only time that the taboo is lifted on touching the fairy thorn. In all other seasons, it must never be interfered with, much less broken or despoiled. But at Bealtaine, groups of young people can go out to the fields and woods and bring back

The best-loved tradition at Bealtaine was to bring home the May blossom.

branches of the sweet-scented blooms and bright yellow marsh marigolds to decorate door lintels and barns, horse harnesses and even the horns of cows. You can still see knots of flowers tied on door knockers on May Day in rural areas and, often, a little sprig of greenery tucked into a carthorse's bridle.

Before Christianity put its foot down and forbade such licentious behaviour, it was the tradition for young men and women to spend the whole of May Eve in the woods together, singing and dancing and coming home in the early morning with their fragrant load of boughs. This is a relic of early fertility rites – by the natural mating of young people at this time of year, it was felt that the land would be encouraged to do likewise. False prudery and imagined sinfulness were far in the future then.

STONE CIRCLES

Many Irish pagan sites are well attended, but there are others now rarely visited. Far to the north in Co. Donegal stands an imposing stone circle on the very top of a windswept hill. Outside the circle, on its eastern side, a single tall grey stone rises from the turf. All around, the countryside stretches away into the misty distance, tiny hedgerows dividing tiny fields. Only the cry of a curlew breaks the silence. What might once have happened here; why was this amphitheatre of standing stones built, with such stupendous effort? The same could be asked of so many of our standing stones, gallauns, circles, rows, passage tombs, dolmens. But here at least there is a clue: The battered signpost that points to this hilltop bears the legend 'Beltany Stone Circle'.

Beltany (or Bealtaine) is clearly a prehistoric site linked to the May Days of the distant past. Down through the centuries, although druids no longer kindle great ritual bonfires here, the knowledge of what this place was intended for remains within folk memory and the language itself.

The wind that soughs through the stones and ripples the long grass on this Donegal hillside might be trying to tell us something, if we knew how to listen. What images of the past might it show us? But Beltany keeps its secrets. It can afford to. It has been here a long time.

The Beltany (or Bealtaine) Stone Circle is a ritual site linked to the great summer festivals of the past.

LUGHNASA: FIRST FRUITS FESTIVAL

It isn't quite dawn yet on this beautiful August morning in Co. Mayo, but the darkness is softening to light grey and the first birds are beginning to twitter. Now, on the mountainside above, a stream of tiny black dots is becoming visible, moving across the slopes towards the summit. As the light strengthens, the flurry of activity down below increases. Men pull on hiking boots, women struggle into rain gear.

This is no easy climb. A good couple of hours and maybe more. Every minute sees increasing numbers of eager pilgrims heading through the gate that leads to the lower slopes, and some, incredibly, are picking their way barefoot over the stones. They look up hopefully to where their fellow climbers have already reached the summit, having left in the middle of the night to watch the sun rise from the top of Croagh Patrick.

Croagh Patrick is one of Ireland's most famous sites of pilgrimage.

> Most of the pilgrims would be surprised to discover that they are continuing a pagan tradition.

Croagh Patrick is one of Ireland's most famous sites of pilgrimage, where on the Sunday closest to the beginning of August, 30,000 or more may make the hazardous ascent. Over the year as a whole, the number is closer to 100,000.

Led by the clergy, with prayers at various stages as well as at the summit, it couldn't be a more Christian observance. Most of the pilgrims would be surprised to discover that they are continuing a pagan tradition. The beginning of August is also the ancient festival of Lughnasa, when people climbed to the highest hilltops to hail the sun god, Lugh, and seek good fortune for the coming harvest.

Archaeological remains on Croagh Patrick show that it was an important ritual site long before Christianity, and so, as its present name suggests, it was given special attention by St Patrick. That redoubtable saint is said to have battled demons on its summit and banished them all, thereby claiming the mountain once and for all for his own religion. In that way the people could continue to climb its slopes, but now they did it as Christians rather than pagans.

CLIMBING TO CROM DUBH

Croagh Patrick isn't the only mountain that is climbed during Lughnasa. Far away to the south west in Co. Kerry, the little village of Cloghane comes alive at the beginning of August each year, with expatriates making special trips home, stalls being set up in the streets, and crowds gathering for the annual ritual of climbing to Crom Dubh. This is the ascent of Mt Brandon, which rises nobly into the sky above Brandon Creek, with an ancient fort on its summit. Today this mountain is linked to St Brendan, but earlier records make it clear that it was formerly known as Bran's Dun, or the fort of Bran, the superhuman seafarer – another example of a Christian saint being superimposed on a pagan deity. Before even Bran, however, this was a landscape closely associated with the earth and harvest god Crom, and it is he who is remembered every year on the last Sunday in July, as young and old make this demanding trek.

THE HUNGRY MONTHS

Modern people tend to regard the summer months as a time of plenty, but in earlier times this was not the case. June and July were known as 'the hungry months', when the carefully hoarded stores from the previous autumn had all been used up over winter, and the new crops and fruits were not yet ripe. Lughnasa isn't a harvest festival, it is a first-fruits celebration, a marking of the eagerly awaited time when there would once more be fresh food on the table. The first sheaf of corn was ceremoniously cut (in later centuries, the first new potatoes dug) and carried to the mountaintop as an offering and propitiation to the pagan sun god Lugh. Today it is still good manners to ask permission of a tree or bush before cutting a branch, as an acknowledgement of our dependence on nature's bounty. To our ancestors, failure to observe this ritual was to invite disaster.

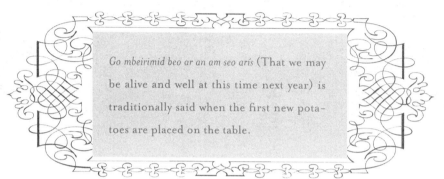

Go mbeirimid beo ar an am seo arís (That we may be alive and well at this time next year) is traditionally said when the first new potatoes are placed on the table.

FROACHAN SUNDAY

Because the hay was usually cut in late July, there was a brief time for gathering together, celebrating with a meal of the first fruits, singing and dancing, before the backbreaking work of saving the harvest. It was also the time to gather *froachans* – the wild bilberries that can be found on Ireland's stony hillsides in August.

Throughout the country you will still find Froachan Sunday celebrated as a time when young men and women set out for the hills to enjoy a day of fun, while gathering canfuls of the tiny blueblack fruits. Young men traditionally make bracelets of the berries for their sweethearts, but these must be left behind on the hill as an offering when it's time to go home. Some fruit should always be brought back to those unable to make the journey into the hills. Many believe that you can forecast the success of the harvest by the size and ripeness of the bilberries on Froachan Sunday.

Nowhere else but at Puck will you find a goat placed on high to indicate that the fair is in progress.

THE GREAT FAIRS

The gathering together of large numbers of people at Lughnasa made them the ideal time for fairs, both for trading and for entertainment. Kings would set their court here for the duration and would hear grievances and administer justice, while buyers and sellers from every corner of Europe would exchange goods and gossip. Intrepid voyagers from the icy wastes of Siberia would spread out their sables and bearskins, while tanned travellers from southern Europe unpacked their priceless packages of sought-after spices and kept an eye out for the best Irish hides and fleeces to take home.

We have convenience stores on every corner now, but we should remember that there was a time when supplies had to be traded or bought at gatherings such as these. Many a housewife must have looked forward impatiently to the great Lughnasa fair, even if it meant walking weary miles there and back.

This was the favoured time too for young couples to 'handfast'. A pillar stone with a hole through its centre was often used for this purpose; there is a fine specimen on Cape Clear Island known as the Cloch na Gealluna (*geall*: a promise). The lovers would clasp hands through the aperture and declare their intention to live together for a year and a day. If, at the following Lughnasa, the couple could not agree, they could separate with no shame or disgrace to either. Any resulting children would be brought up by the woman's family.

OULD LAMMAS FAIR

One of the oldest gatherings still going strong today is the Ould Lammas Fair at Ballycastle, Co. Antrim (Lammas, from 'loaf mass' or the first bread baked from the new grain). As the traditional song has it:

> *At the Ould Lammas Fair boys, were you ever there,*
> *Were you ever at the Fair in Ballycastle-o?*
> *Did you treat your Mary Ann*
> *To some dulse and yellow man*
> *At the Ould Lammas Fair in Ballycastle-o!*

(Dulse is the seaweed gathered and eaten as a delicacy around the Irish coastline, while 'yellow man' is a particularly sticky sweet still made and sold at the Ballycastle gathering.)

PUCK FAIR

It's a fine August evening in Killorglin, Co. Kerry. The crowds have been pushing into the square for hours and now there isn't enough room to slip a blade of grass between them. A hush falls as the little girl dressed in white robes comes forward, the golden crown held carefully in her hands. Raising it on high she speaks the ritual words in both Irish and English. The crown is lowered and placed on the horns of a wild mountain goat. He is held securely by a couple of local men well versed in the pugnacious ways of goats, but he seems placid enough as he receives the honour. Rousing cheers break from the crowds, music strikes up, and the festivities are under way. King Puck (*puc*, wild goat) rides in his ceremonial chariot to be hoisted up to the high platform where he will be fêted and fed for the next three days before being released back to his mountainside.

Puck Fair is probably the oldest surviving celebration of its kind in Ireland today, and, remarkably, it is still held on the same days it has always been. In other areas, fairs have moved throughout the centuries to more convenient weekend dates, shifting each year, but Puck continues to be held on 10th–12th August. In pre-Gregorian Calendar days, those would have been 1st–3rd August, or Lughnasa. The three days have been known since time immemorial as Gathering Day, Fair Day and Scattering Day. A charter from 1603 by King James I grants legal status to the already ancient fair.

English charter fairs were often characterised by the hanging up of a glove or similar symbol, to indicate that the official law of

The crown is placed on the horns of a
wild mountain goat, known as King Puck.

the gathering was in force, superseding any other local legislation for the duration of the event. Nowhere else but at Puck, though, will you find a huge and threateningly horned wild mountain goat crowned and placed on high to indicate that the fair is in progress. That is one of the few direct survivals from pre-Christian days, a joyous acknowledgement of the pagan symbol of fertility.

'It was the highlight of the summer, our parents taking us to Puck,' remembers Sandra, a young mother. 'We'd get some pennies to spend on sweets and we'd be running everywhere, looking at the horses, the cattle, the people. And to see the goat being crowned, that was the best of all! We thought it was wonderful to see a goat up there being treated like a king! I'll be taking my own children this year, carrying on the tradition.'

'The main thing was the anticipation,' recalls Ivor, a public relations executive. 'You'd hear that the fair was on its way and you couldn't wait. There was a parade on the first day and the older boys took part in it with their spears and leather outfits, but for us younger ones, any time not spent at the fair was time badly spent!'

LOUGH DERG: PENANCE OR PAGANISM?

Another event occurs around Lughnasa each year, although it could hardly be called a celebration. In late July and August, pilgrims throng to tiny Station Island on the remote and mysterious Lough Derg to endure three days of harsh penitential observances. These include staying awake for the first night and all the next day, fasting for twenty-four hours, circling the stony ground of the island barefoot while saying prayers, and generally experiencing discomfort at the level usually reserved for trainee commandos. Yet the pilgrims not only survive, but many come back again, year after year.

In pre-Christian times, there was a belief that here, at the edge of the known world, was an entrance to the Otherworld. Originally it would have been used by druids in their search for illumination and wisdom; they undertook severe trials such as starvation, isolation and sleep deprivation to extend their powers.

Later, it was a place where the wealthy could themselves endure the starvation/sleeplessness ordeal. By experiencing the Christian Purgatory now, they believed, they could reduce the amount of penance due after death. The earliest maps of Ireland sometimes show Lough Derg and nowhere else, indicating its renown. Martin Behaim's world map of 1492 is one such example. There is certainly evidence of priests complaining to Rome about the charges levied at Lough Derg in medieval times. So popular did it become that several popes tried to close it down.

Early documents record a mysterious cave at Lough Derg. Guillebert de Lannoy, in his *Voyages et Ambassades* of 1430, made a cryptic reference to a second, by that time forbidden, cavern:

> *At the end of this cave, in which I was shut up for 2 or 3 hours, they say is a mouth of another cave, but St Patrick stopped it with a stone which he placed upon it, and it is still there ...*

There was a belief that here, at the edge of the known world, was an entrance to the Otherworld.

The permitted cave is clearly marked (as 'Caverna Purgatory') in Fr Thomas Carve's *Lyra Hibernica*, dating from 1666. Here visions were seen, both hideous and beautiful. Some spoke of strange vapours that put you into a trance. Today, alas, that cave (and any further passages which may once have led off it) lies buried beneath the massive dome of the church that dominates the tiny island. It is unlikely that any concealed entrance, any locked trapdoor could be found under the massive weight of limestone and marble, polished wood and wrought iron. Whatever lies hidden keeps its secrets.

St Patrick, we are told, fought some of his most demanding battles at Lough Derg, conquering a fearful serpent and imprisoning it forever in the lake. As we have seen, a saint taking on a serpent or dragon is always an attack by Christianity on pagan beliefs. Thereafter the island was given the name of St Patrick's Purgatory. Old boatmen say the serpent comes out during storms and lashes her tail across the lake, showing she's still there, just biding her time.

The island on Lough Derg is a strange, brooding, almost threatening place when viewed from the embarkation pier on the mainland. The church and associated buildings so completely cover the little islet that they look to be floating in the water. Casual visitors are not allowed. You go there on pilgrimage for the full three days or you don't go at all.

And yet pilgrims praise the Lough Derg experience as one of enormous peace and happiness. 'I loved it. It was so peaceful, and you had time to think,' says one. 'I went because I needed an answer to something really important, and I got it,' says another. 'I went with a special request and promised I'd go back if it was granted, and it was, and I did!' says a third.

Druids seeking enlightenment, pilgrims seeking answers? Perhaps the island on Lough Derg hasn't changed its nature very much after all. We've just changed the way we express our beliefs.

For many, the Lough Derg pilgrimage brings
peace and happiness.

The Winter & Summer Solstices

Many of our main stone circles are, in fact, ancient observatories built to keep track of the sun as it travels through its lowest and highest points. These special days – the winter and summer solstices, or equinoxes – were always significant.

MIDWINTER: THE TURNING OF THE YEAR

Around the third week in December in western Europe, the sun reaches its lowest point and the nights are at their longest. It is a time when most of us yearn for a sign that the earth is at last turning again towards the light. Once the turning point of the shortest day had passed, our ancestors celebrated by sharing out the precious hoard of fruit, grain and salted meat, to honour the returning sun god. It's an instinctive feeling of relief and celebration, so deeply rooted in our instinct that the Christian Church had not a hope of eradicating it. Instead it placed one of the most sacred of its own celebrations, the birth of the Christ Child, at this time. And so today we still gather special foodstuffs, hold feasts and give gifts to celebrate birth, rebirth and the turning of the year.

In Ireland, there is one tradition that stretches back unbroken as far as records go and beyond. A custom that is so strange in its outward appearance that observers have been at a loss to understand its true meaning, often dismissing it as some wild, unmeaning peasant revelry. But there's more to it than that.

THE WREN, THE WREN!

It's 26th December, a wild and windy morning on the Dingle Peninsula in Kerry. Grey waves lash the rocks along the seashore, and gulls soar on the updraft like floating flakes of foam. In Britain, they call it Boxing Day; in Ireland, St Stephen's Day. In either country, it's often a time for recovering from over-indulgence, perhaps by going out for a long, healthy walk.

But there aren't too many folk abroad at this hour. Even Dingle's windswept quayside is empty, and the front doors of brightly painted cottages are not hospitably ajar, as usual, but firmly shut.

All is not quite as it seems, however. Walk up that street and push open the door of that pub. Inside, the place is packed with people of all ages. Two women, still in their raincoats, pour tea from vast urns, and the bar is doing a roaring trade in pints. The ancient flagstones, worn smooth by generations, are covered with a layer of bright golden straw that gives off the evocative scent of August harvests.

On a battered wooden table, men pull long stalks from bundled sheaves, each stalk still holding its rich bounty of grain. Six or seven stalks are bunched together and handed to the leader, who is working quickly, twisting each handful in turn onto a length of rough string that has been tied between a wall hook and the nearest pillar. When it is judged long enough, this string is taken off. It is now a golden cloak of grain, which is donned by one of

The wren boys, in motley clothes and straw cloaks, go from house to house singing and dancing.

the men. Another pair of skilful hands is putting the finishing touches to a woven headdress of straw with a delicate cage on top, in which is placed a small plastic bird.

Nearby a mother and daughter apply black greasepaint to a young man's face, while two more youths wait their turn.

Up at the bar stands a tall creature, wearing a battered old black frock coat, heavy boots and a woven wicker head. The head sports a curving, cruel beak of split cow's horn, and a crest of crow feathers from poll to nape. Even as you pause to stare, the creature lifts a bottle and carefully pours a libation down its cowhorn beak to refresh the man within.

Yet it's not funny. It stirs the deepest part of our instincts. In all of this – the weaving of the sheaves, the fashioning of straw headdresses, the strange half-bird half-man – we are seeing echoes of the ancient past. At the turning point of the year, people must disguise

A skilfully woven wicker headdress completes this wren boy's disguise.

themselves and display a wren on a branch of prickly furze. Once it would have been a real wren, captured and killed for this special day. Today's pragmatic Wren Boys may take the handy option of a Christmas ornament – and if this happens to be a robin rather than a wren, what matter?

The musicians have been playing for half an hour, their notes barely audible in the din. But now a huge drum beats a warning tattoo and instantly there is a frenzy of cheering, cries of encouragement, and everyone presses eagerly towards the door. The Wren Boys are abroad.

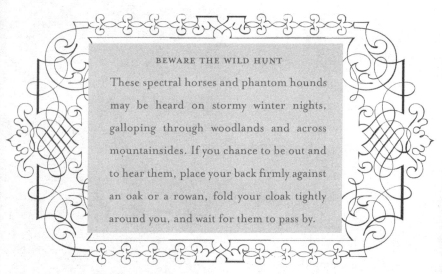

BEWARE THE WILD HUNT

These spectral horses and phantom hounds may be heard on stormy winter nights, galloping through woodlands and across mountainsides. If you chance to be out and to hear them, place your back firmly against an oak or a rowan, fold your cloak tightly around you, and wait for them to pass by.

They parade down the main road, led by a dancing figure dressed as a white mare. Visitors, swept up in the excitement, colour their faces with borrowed crayons and join in this age-old ritual. The parade passes the church, drums beating an atavistic summons that predates Christianity in this island by thousands of years. In the graveyard, white plaster statues watch impassively as the colourful pagan ritual passes by, and the old chant rings out:

The wren, the wren, the king of all birds,
St Stephen's Day was caught in the furze,
Up with the kettle and down with the pan,
Give us a penny to bury the wran!

KING OF THE BIRDS

When all the birds of the air met together to decide who should be king, it was agreed that whoever flew the highest should be chosen. All set off, but gradually fell back one by one. Only the eagle flew on and upwards on his powerful wings. When he had reached the limit of his strength, he cried in triumph, 'I am king!' But a tiny wren had hidden away in the feathers of the great eagle's neck. He flew out and, rising a few feet higher, chirped,

The parade passes the church, drums beating an atavistic summons that predates Christianity in Ireland.

'No, *I* am king, I have flown the highest!' And from that day on, the wren has been known as king of all birds.

Long before the legend was recorded, the wren was already credited with unique magical powers that made him first among his peers. This was recognised by the druids, who incorporated the little bird into their own rituals of foretelling the future. But why does the Wren Day ritual require the killing and displaying of this acknowledged king? Wouldn't that be inviting misfortune?

Not when it takes place around the winter solstice. Just as all growth disappears underground at this time of year, the old king must disappear. Only with his death does spring and rebirth become possible. That is why symbols of fertility abound in the procession: the white mare leading represents the fertility of the earth goddess, the golden cloaks worn by the players are heavy with the grain of last autumn's harvest.

As long as human beings have prayed for fertility, both for themselves and for their fields, different versions of this death and rebirth drama have been played out. But in more savage times, instead of the tiny but mighty wren being killed, the sacrifice may well have been human, the ceremonial execution of a young man who had been king for the year.

ST STEPHEN'S DAY

Naturally enough, the Christian Church sought to stamp out such traditions but found it impossible. So they did the next best thing: planted a saint's day associated with sacrifice – St Stephen was the first Christian martyr – on top of the pagan festival and then decried the old ritual as children's nonsense. They even demonised

the wren, creating a myth in which he was responsible for betraying St Stephen to his pursuers. This treachery, then, became the new explanation for killing the wren at Christmas-tide.

Whenever you find a saint's day associated with an old pagan tradition, you can be sure of a power struggle taking place. And whenever a particular bird or animal is accused of anti-Christian behaviour, it is a good idea to look more closely at the older associations with that creature. Horns and cloven hooves, after all, were powerful and beloved symbols of nature deities at one time.

The procession is turning back towards the pub now, the collection boxes for a local charity already pleasantly heavy. From a dripping bush, a genuine wren scolds vociferously. Maybe he's offended that they're using Christmas robin ornaments instead of himself?

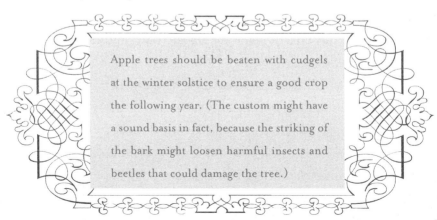

Apple trees should be beaten with cudgels at the winter solstice to ensure a good crop the following year. (The custom might have a sound basis in fact, because the striking of the bark might loosen harmful insects and beetles that could damage the tree.)

MIDSUMMER: BONFIRES ON THE HILLS

Passengers on a plane flying into Cork Airport on a June evening are perplexed. Is it a fog? Low-lying cloud? Everywhere there are wreaths and columns of smoke, some pale grey, some so dark as to be almost black, twisting their way up into the serene summer sky. It can be seen everywhere, but particularly across the city. The sight is unearthly, like a scene from Dante's *Inferno* or Tolkien's *The Lord of the Rings*.

Driving up through housing estates on the hilly northside of Cork, there is definitely something afoot. Children are running from every direction, dragging old planks, scraps of timber, bundles of newspaper. Bigger youths are hauling broken tables and armchairs that have seen better days, and adding them to towering pyres that are growing rapidly on open patches of waste ground. Everybody is busy, excited, shouting and laughing as they work. Elderly folk bring chairs to their front doors and settle down for what is clearly a spectator event.

'It's the busiest night in the year for us,' says a fire officer gloomily. 'By the time it's dark, we'll be chasing all over the place, dealing with fires that have got out of hand.'

And indeed as dusk falls around 10pm or later – the evenings are long at this time of year – the smoke from hundreds of fires can be seen all over the city.

So what is the reason for this sudden outburst, on this particular date? It's not Halloween, nor Christmas, nor the celebration of a famous victory. It is 23rd June, known also as St John's Eve, which is the nearest Christian festival to the midsummer solstice of 21st June, and the ancient Celtic custom of bonfire-building is in full swing.

RITUAL FIRE-MAKING

The fire honours the sun at its highest point. It had to be lit at sunset and tended until midnight had passed, and ancient communities gathered on hilltops, rocky outcrops or at crossroads specifically for this purpose. Young men and women joined hands and jumped through the flames to mark their 'handfasting', or official betrothal. Farmers leapt as high as they could, so their crops would grow tall. A married couple might leap in the hope that the sun god would bless their union with a baby. Youths seized burning sticks and tossed them into the air as high as possible – then ducked the showers of sparks. Next day, the bonfire's cold ashes were sprinkled in the fields. If the whole ritual were not observed by the community, their crops might fail, animals die, or salmon fail to come upriver that year.

In 21st-century Cork, as dark settles over the city and the fires die down, daring young boys and girls run and leap across the glowing embers, encouraged by the cheers and clapping of their friends. Maybe they think they are the first ever to do such a thing. They may have no idea that they are enacting a sun-worshipping ritual in a modern city – they know only that they've always done it, as have their parents, grandparents and great-grandparents before them.

Finally, the smallest children, nodding wearily, are taken home to bed. The others follow, blackened, dirty, happy. Fire engines patrol the city, watching for stray sparks. Another Bonfire Night is over.

Part Three

Traditions in Story

THE THREE SORROWS

OF STORYTELLING

In ancient times, a well-told story might go on all night, depending on comments from the crowd.

Once Upon A Time ...

he storyteller's voice is soft, hypnotic, the gentle Irish rolling smoothly off his tongue. The audience, packed into a small schoolroom, is spellbound, adults and children alike. Slowly he weaves the tale of the lonely farmer, the strange golden ball he finds and hides in the chimney, the beautiful young girl who comes to work for him, and the frightening visitor who rides in at midnight.

'His horse's hooves striking sparks out of the stones,' he says. 'Into the room with him, and he stops in the middle of the floor.' In the dramatic pause that follows, you could hear a pin drop. Then he lowers his voice to a near-whisper: '*Ní bhainimse leis an saol seo, tagaim ón saol eile* (I am not of this life, I come from the Otherworld)'.

A collective sigh arises from the people, and they nod slowly. This is as it should be. The storyteller has them in the palm of his hand now. He leads the story up and around and about, and finally to its happy ending. There is the tribute of a full five seconds of enraptured silence before the applause takes over.

Diarmuid Ó Drisceoil is a *scéalaí,* or storyteller, and historian, and this is the annual Cape Clear Storytelling Festival. Participants come from all over the world, while the local ferry companies lay on extra sailings and the pubs stock up on supplies. Tales are told in English as well as Irish, by New Yorkers as well as Kerrymen and Galwegians, but all are part of the same creative process that brings legends to life and connects story, storyteller and audience in the oldest, most satisfying way.

AN ANCIENT ART

The art of storytelling is still alive in Ireland, and not just at special festivals. Anywhere a few are gathered, someone will always have a tale to tell, and everyone settles down to listen. It's an old custom. Back in ancient Ireland, poets recounted great battles or recited the genealogy of the noble family under whose roof they were being sheltered. Well-loved tales of Cúchulainn, of Fionn Mac Cumhaill, of the Red Branch Knights and Queen Maeve, were told in great halls by the blazing log fire, as the winds howled, the rain pattered on the roof, and the audience crowded closer to hear every word.

The ancient tales of Ireland are meant to be recounted by the human voice and heard by the human ear. They were not designed to be read page by page, the book perhaps being casually put down

The ancient tales of Ireland are meant to be recounted by the human voice and heard by the human ear.

with a marker showing where you had left off. They were never intended for computer screens. They were an experience in which everyone shared – whether they laughed, wept or mourned.

A well-told story might go on all night, with digressions added, depending on comments from the crowd. It could take several different directions, depending on whose family needed to be praised or discredited for the occasion. (Just as Shakespeare discreetly ended his *Henry VIII* with the birth of Elizabeth, omitting any mention of the later beheading of Elizabeth's mother, so too would an Irish bard adjust his tale for his patron.)

For thousands of years, the legends and stories of Ireland, royal genealogies and records of major events were passed down in the oral tradition, through the songs, poems, epic declamations of druids, bards and poets. Being able to recall a complete family history with marriages and intermarriages, recite the stirring events of a great battle, or relate how the Tuatha Dé Danann vanquished the Fomorians was the skill of those who had trained their memories for many years. The direct descendants of these are the traditional storytellers, who still enjoy a devoted following throughout Ireland.

Over the centuries, one rule has always held firm: You are not a true *scéalaí* unless you have in your memory, and can relate at the drop of a hat, in every detail, the Three Sorrows of Storytelling. This is the collective name for three stories: *The Quest of the Children of Turenn*, *The Fate of the Sons of Usna*, and *The Enchantment of the Children of Lir*.

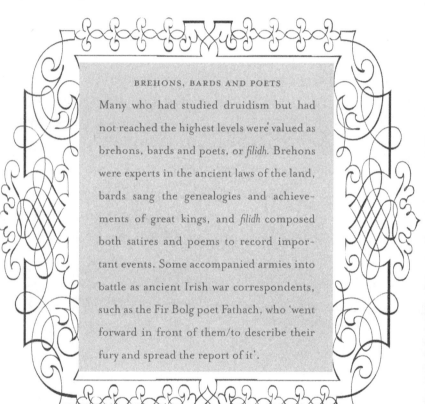

BREHONS, BARDS AND POETS

Many who had studied druidism but had not reached the highest levels were valued as brehons, bards and poets, or *filidh*. Brehons were experts in the ancient laws of the land, bards sang the genealogies and achievements of great kings, and *filidh* composed both satires and poems to record important events. Some accompanied armies into battle as ancient Irish war correspondents, such as the Fir Bolg poet Fathach, who 'went forward in front of them/to describe their fury and spread the report of it'.

Three Sorrowful Tales

We cannot date any one of this trio of heart-breaking legends with any accuracy. All we can be sure of is that they had been narrated and heard, held in oral memory and handed down, long before Christianity came to Ireland. When finally committed to writing by monks who rightly felt that such rich heritage deserved to be recorded, inevitably they underwent some alteration, as the Church expunged those sections that appeared too pagan, or introduced a suitably religious motif into the main plot.

Within the Three Sorrows, as in all the old stories, gods sometimes appear as men, queens deal in witchcraft, kings are merely spoiled, bad-tempered children. Historic periods are telescoped, drawn out, mixed up. The hero of one tale will suddenly turn up in another to lend a hand; episodes from an entirely different era or legend may be interpolated. It's all part of the rich pattern of storytelling. All three of these tales illuminate in their own unique way the culture of the ancient peoples of Ireland.

Read the stories aloud. Then re-tell them to children and friends. Adjust the detail, add something for the occasion or the audience. In so doing, you are part of an ancient tradition.

The first, *The Quest of the Children of Turenn*, shows how loyalty to one's clan was paramount, and how a breach could lead to disaster. It incorporates travel legends, gathered no doubt from traders who came from distant lands to buy and sell on the shores of Ireland. It also shows the importance of honour and the rigorous law of the *geasa*, or obligation, which, once laid upon a man, must be fulfilled. It is the longest of the Three Sorrowful Tales.

The second, *The Fate of the Sons of Usna,* is possibly the greatest love story of ancient Ireland, foreshadowing the causes of that later mighty battle featured in the *Táin*. As well as love everlasting, this tale champions loyalty and honour and highlights the shame of breaking promises.

The third, *The Enchantment of the Children of Lir,* is certainly the best-known and perhaps the most beloved of Irish legends, passed down from generation to generation and as familiar to today's toddlers in kindergarten as to their great-great-great-grandparents. Here, the later Christian interpolations have been omitted, and the tale is told as the pagan bards of ancient Ireland might have recounted it.

The First:
The Quest of the Children of Turenn

Once upon a time and a long time ago it was, when the Tuatha Dé Danann ruled Ireland, their people were dreadfully harassed by sea-pirates called the Fomorians. These fellows had a base on Tory Island off Donegal, and that was too close altogether, for they were constantly descending on the country, carrying off young women and men as slaves. And if that wasn't bad enough, they imposed cruel taxes as well: Would you believe there was a tax on every quern for grinding corn, every kneading trough for making dough, and every flagstone for baking bread? A poll-tax there was too, an ounce of gold on the head of every man, and if it wasn't paid, then that was the worse for you, because they cut off your nose. Those were unhappy times indeed, and the people prayed for someone to stand up to these wicked pirates ...

The right man comes at the right time, they say, and that was the case here. Far away a young man was growing up. Lugh Lámh Fada, or Lugh of the Long Arm, was his name, and he was the son of the lordly Cian, one of the Tuatha Dé Danann, who had married a princess of the Fomorians named Ethlinn. A beautiful young man he was, strong in body and brilliant in mind, for the Immortal Ones had seen to it that he should have both lordship and authority in full measure, and whatever he set his mind to do, that thing was done.

Living on an isle in the western sea, he was taught by the sea-god Manannán Mac Lir and made ready for warfare or for kingship, when his day should come to work the will of the Wise Ones on earth. And so it was that he came to hear of the unhappy plight of the Dé Danann in Ireland.

'This is what I was born to do,' said Lugh at once. 'To rescue the people of Éireann and my own father, too, from this tyranny.'

So, with Manannán's blessing, Lugh took arms, mounted his magical steed, called his friends about him, and rode across the sea to the shores of his homeland.

As it happened, on that very day the chiefs of the Tuatha Dé Danann had assembled at Tara to meet with the tax collectors of the Fomorians. While they waited, they saw a bright company coming from the west, led by a young man whose face was so radiant that they could hardly look upon it. Riding on a white horse he was, with a great sword at his side and a helmet set with precious stones on his head. While the Dé Danann were welcoming these strangers, another band came into view from the north. Nine times nine was their number, and they were fierce and dark of countenance. They were the Fomorians, come to collect their

Riding on a white horse was Lugh, with a great sword at his side.

tribute. Arrogantly they came, and the Dé Danann rose to their feet to do them honour.

Lugh (for it was he on the white horse) was greatly surprised at this and asked why honour was shown to such unworthy characters.

'We have no choice,' said the High King, 'for if even a child stayed seated, they would use that excuse to attack and kill every one of us.'

This seemed very wrong to Lugh and he gave the command to his own followers, who immediately rushed on the Fomorians and slew all but nine. These nine were brought before Lugh, who sent them back to their king with this message: 'Let him seek homage and tribute wherever he will, but he will get no more from Ireland!'

Then these Fomorians hastened northwards, and the people of Danu made Lugh their captain of war, for they knew that the Fomorian king would soon seek to avenge this insult. As indeed he did, for he was none other than Balor of the Evil Eye, whose wife was the dreaded Caithlin of the Twisted Teeth. Swiftly Balor assembled a great host of his sea-pirates and prepared the war-ships. The northern seas were white with the foam of their oars as they swept down upon the land that had dared to defy them.

'When you have destroyed every being in Éireann,' roared Balor to his war leaders, 'tie the island itself to your ships and drag it north, far into the desolation of ice and snow. Then it will trouble us no longer!'

In the meantime, Lugh gathered his forces on all sides and sent his father, Cian, to rouse the fairy warriors of the *sidhe* to come to their aid also. But when Cian was on his way to do this, what should he see but three armed warriors coming towards him. These were the Sons of Turenn, namely Brian, Iuchar and Iucharba. There was an ancient feud between their house and that of Cian, and their people were bound to fight whenever they met. Cian, being alone, knew he could not fight three, but having druidic skills, he turned himself into a wild pig and joined a herd that was rooting in the trees close by.

The Sons of Turenn wondered what had happened to the distant warrior they had seen riding towards them, and Brian suspected some trickery. His brothers could not think what to do, but Brian laughed at their stupidity and struck them with a druidic wand, so that they became fierce hounds. In this shape, they soon discovered Cian in his disguise. In pig form but with human voice, Cian asked for mercy. Iuchar and Iucharba were willing to grant this, but Brian was not.

'I swear by the wind and by the sun that if you had seven lives, I would take them all!' he said. Then Cian asked that he might at least turn himself back into the shape of a man before being killed, and this was granted.

'Now I have the better of you,' Cian said. 'For killing a pig you would have had to pay a pig's price, but now you will have to pay the honour price of a man, and a great man at that. And I tell you now that never was there a greater honour price in this land, than the one you will have to pay.'

'And who will tell what we have done, when you are dead?' enquired Brian scornfully.

'I am Cian of the Tuatha Dé Danann, and the very weapons you use will cry out against you.'

'Then we will use the stones of the earth,' said Brian, and there-upon they picked up great rocks from the ground and rained them upon Cian until he died. Then they tried to bury him, but six times the earth would not take his body and cast it out again. The seventh time, they left the body lying and piled the rocks over it to hide their deed. And then they rode on to Tara, for they, too, were joining the army that would fight the Fomorians.

The battle against the Fomorians was successful, and they were driven from the shores of Ireland, but afterwards Lugh realised that he had not seen his father during the conflict. When he asked his comrades, they had not seen him either, and he was not to be found among the dead.

'If he were alive, he would be here,' said Lugh, 'and I swear by the gods of my people that I will not eat or drink until I know what has befallen my father.'

The stones under which Cian was buried cried out and told of his murder.

'I swear by the gods of my people that I will not eat or drink until I know what has befallen my father.'

And it so happened that they were passing the place where Cian had been murdered, and the stones under which he was buried cried out and told of the deed. Lugh searched and found his father's body.

'That a man of the Danu should be killed by one of his fellow men!' he cried. 'I am sick to the heart to see this. My eyes are blinded, my ears are deafened.' And he grieved long and bitterly. Then he laid Cian in an honoured grave, set a pillar stone thereon with his name carved in ogham, and sang a lament for him. And this was the right and proper thing for a noble young man to do for his father.

After that Lugh returned to Tara and was placed in honour on the king's right hand for the feast celebrating the victory. Lugh looked round about him and saw, among all the princes and lords of the Danann folk, the Sons of Turenn sitting among the assembly. They were among the strongest and the handsomest of those who were present at that time, and they had borne themselves right bravely in the fight with the Fomorians. Lugh asked of the king that the chain of silence might be shaken, and when the assembly fell quiet, he said:

'O king, and ye princes of the People of Danu, I ask what vengeance would each of you exact upon a man who had foully murdered your father?'

The whole assembly was shocked, and the king said:

'Surely it is not the father of Lugh Lámh Fada who has thus been slain?'

'It is so,' was Lugh's reply, 'and those who did the deed are listening to me now, and know it better than I.'

'Not in one day would I slay the murderer of my father,' said the king fiercely, 'but I would tear from him a limb day by day till he were dead.'

And so said all the lords of the Dananns, and the Sons of Turenn among the rest, for they were sure no-one could know of their secret deed.

'They have sentenced themselves, the murderers of my father,' said Lugh. 'Nevertheless I shall accept an *eric*, or blood fine, from them, and if they will pay it, it shall be well – but if not, let them beware.'

Brian was unwilling to confess but his two brothers said, 'Clearly he has discovered it is us. Do you confess because you are the eldest? If you do not, then we shall.'

So Brian rose up and said: 'It is to us you have spoken, Lugh, since you know there is enmity from olden times between our houses. Declare our fine and we shall pay it.'

And so Lugh announced the fine the Sons of Turenn would pay for killing his father, and this is the list he gave:

Three apples
The skin of a pig

A spear
Two steeds and a chariot
Seven swine
A whelp of a dog
A cooking spit
Three shouts on a hill

'This doesn't sound too heavy a fine,' said the Sons of Turenn, although their hearts told them that there was more in this than appeared at first hearing. And they were right to think so, as you will see. But they gave their word and entered into agreement with Lugh and with the High King that the eric should be paid to fully compensate for the death of Cian. And then Lugh told them the truth of the obligation, or *geasa*, that had been laid on them.

'The three apples grow in the garden of the Hesperides, in the east of the world, and none but these will do, for they are magical. Bright gold in colour and as large as the head of a child, their taste is of honey. They will heal any evil disease, and may be eaten many times but never grow less. Not easy will be your task, for those who guard them know the ancient prophecy that one day three knights from the western world will come and attempt to steal them.

'The skin of the pig belongs to the king of Greece. Laid upon a wounded man it will make him whole and well, if only he be still breathing. Pass it through a stream, and the water will be made wine for nine days after. Valued highly is that skin, as you may imagine. And do ye know what is the spear that I demanded?'

The three magical apples grow in the garden of the Hesperides, in the east of the world.

'We do not,' said the Sons of Turenn.

'It is the poisoned spear of the king of Persia. Luin is its name, and so fierce is its rage that it must be kept in a pot of soothing herbs or it would fly out to deal death on all around. And do ye know what are the two horses and the chariot ye must get?'

'We do not know,' said they, feeling ever more certain that they had let themselves in for great trouble and danger.

'The steeds and the chariot belong to Dobar, king of Sicily. They are magical creatures that can travel over land or sea, and cannot be killed by any weapon. And the seven pigs belong to Asal, king of the Golden Pillars, and they may be eaten every night, and the next morning they are alive again. And the hound-whelp I asked of you belongs to the king of Iorroway. She can catch and slay any beast in the world, and you will not get her easily. The cooking spit is one that the fairy women of the Island of Finchory have in their kitchen, and that island is not to be found either on land or on sea. And the hill on which ye must give three shouts is that of Mochaen in the north of Loughlann. Mochaen and his sons will permit no man to raise a shout upon their hill. With him it was that my father was trained to arms, and if I forgave ye his death, yet would Mochaen not forgive it. And now ye know the eric which ye have to pay for the slaying of Cian, my father.'

Now indeed were the Sons of Turenn dismayed, and they went home to tell the tidings to their father.

'This is bad indeed,' said Turenn. 'I see death and doom coming from that eric, and perhaps that is only as it should be. Yet if Lugh or Manannán will help you, you may yet succeed. Go and ask Lugh for the loan of the fairy steed on which he rode here to Éireann. He will refuse, for it was a loan to him from Manannán. Then ask for the loan of *Scuab Toinne*, or *Wave Sweeper*, the magic boat of Manannán, and he will have to give that to you, for he may not refuse a second request.'

And it happened exactly as he said, and so the Sons of Turenn launched *Wave Sweeper* from the shores of Ireland, while their sister, Eithne, wept at their going. 'Don't weep,' they told her. 'Better to be killed a hundred times over than to meet the death of cowards.'

'Which way do we go now?' asked Iuchar.

'That is easily answered,' said Brian, and he whispered, 'Take us swiftly, Boat of Manannán, to the Garden of the Hesperides.'

The spirit of the boat leapt forward across the ocean so that in no long time they drew nigh to the coast where was the far-famed garden of the Golden Apples.

Iuchar and Iucharba were for fighting their way in and snatching the apples, but Brian took more careful thought. Striking himself and each of his brothers with a druid wand, he changed them all into strong-winged hawks, and they flew into the garden. The guardians of the apples threw showers of arrows and darts, but the hawks evaded all of these until none were left, and then each seized an apple in his talons. But Brian seized two, for he took one in his beak as well. Then they flew as swiftly as they might towards the shore.

Now the ruler of the Garden of the Hesperides had three daughters, and he transformed these into three griffins, who pursued the hawks, casting darts of fire at them. But Brian changed himself and his brothers into three swans, and they plunged into the sea, and the burning darts were quenched. Then the griffins gave over the chase, and the Sons of Turenn made for their magic boàt and embarked with the four apples. Thus was their first quest ended.

To get the pigskin from the king of Greece, the Sons of Turenn disguised themselves as bards, since such learned men are always received with honour. And indeed they were made welcome. First the minstrels of the king sang songs, then came the turn of the Irish bards. Now the Sons of Turenn were warriors, not poets,

'Better to be killed a hundred times over
than to meet the death of cowards.'

259

and were hard pressed to think of something. Brian did his best, and recited a poem praising the king and laying special emphasis on the magic pigskin:

> *O king, your fame is so great,*
> *Like to a mighty oak tree,*
> *The thing that is surely thy fate*
> *For a cloak, give thy pigskin to me!*

'Not to all the poets of the world would I give that pigskin,' said the king. 'But I honour men of learning, and I will instead give you the fill of the skin in red gold, three times over. How does that suit you?'

Brian's brothers looked at each other, worried, but Brian bowed low to the king, thanking him for his generosity. They all went to the treasure house to measure out the gold, then suddenly Brian snatched the skin. The three Sons of Turenn fought their way out and down to the shore where the boat took them swiftly away, and the pigskin healed the wounds they had received in the struggle. And thus was the second quest of the Sons of Turenn ended.

'Time now to seek the poisoned spear that is in Persia,' said Brian. And straightaway the boat took them to that very land. And since the disguise of poets worked so well in Greece, they decided to try the same ruse again – although it has to be said that Iuchar and Iucharba were less keen than Brian, since they hadn't an idea in their heads of how to compose a poem. But they all dressed their hair in the manner of Irish poets and were admitted to the palace of King Pisear. As they were being led through the courtyard, they saw the spear, Luin, resting in its pot of calming herbs and noted its position carefully.

Once more they listened politely to the lays sung by the king's minstrel and, after that, it was Brian's turn. He was getting a bit better at it by this time, and he recited this:

> *Pisear cares not for any spear,*
> *Not while he has this weapon here,*
> *Let enemies come, as they may,*
> *This poisoned dart will all them slay.*
> *The yew is truly king of woods,*
> *No other tree can lay a claim,*
> *This shining shaft, with deadly point,*
> *Flying fiercely forth, will always maim.*

'That's a nice enough poem,' said the king of Persia, 'but I'm not quite sure why you bring my spear into it.'

'Well, now that you ask,' replied Brian courteously, 'it is that selfsame spear I would like as a reward for my fine poem.'

'Indeed and you will not!' said the king fiercely. 'It's death you deserve for even daring to ask!'

And he stood up to call his guards and have the Sons of Turenn arrested. But Brian flung the fourth golden apple that he had taken from the Garden of the Hesperides, and it dashed out the king's brains.

Immediately the brothers all drew their swords and made for the courtyard, seizing the magic spear as they went. It took a bit of time and a bit of fighting, but eventually they escaped to

Wave Sweeper, which immediately took them out and beyond the Ninth Wave to safety, while they healed their wounds from the fighting with the magic pigskin. And thus ended the third quest of the Sons of Turenn.

Now where had they got to? They had the golden apples of the Hesperides, they had the pigskin of Greece, and they had the spear of Persia. That was three of the eight things on Lugh's list, and having got this far they began to be a bit more cheerful and think that they just might survive and win the day. And so they sailed away merrily to the island of Sicily to see could they get the two horses and the chariot of King Dobar. *Wave Sweeper* bore them swiftly and smoothly, and indeed it's hard to know how they could have managed any of the adventures at all if they hadn't had that boat belonging to Manannán Mac Lir.

Brian's two brothers refused absolutely to try the poet trick again, for they felt it was undignified for warriors to pretend to such artistic activities. It was thus agreed that they would be mercenary soldiers instead. It was often the custom for young Irishmen who were not allied to one noble house or another to seek service with foreign kings, so it wouldn't be seen as anything unusual in Sicily. And so, when they arrived, they strode with great confidence to the royal palace and found the king and his lords in the garden, enjoying the fine evening that was in it. Bending the knee and offering homage, as was fitting, the Sons of Turenn requested the king to take them for military service and were accepted.

A month went by, and another half a month, and they were kept busy with this and that on the king's business, but never a sign did they see of the horses or the chariot.

Now where had they got to? They had the golden apples of the Hesperides, they had the pigskin of Greece, and they had the spear of Persia.

'What will we do now?' Iuchar and Iucharba asked Brian.

He thought about it for a moment. 'Attack is the best method. Let us go fully armed and prepared for marching, and tell Dobar that we're leaving unless we see his famous steeds.'

'Why didn't you say so before?' said the king when he heard the Sons of Turenn's request. 'Tomorrow is a big festival day, and you'll see them then if you only take the trouble to turn up.'

They were there bright and early, as you'd imagine, and saw the steeds yoked and the chariot driven round a great plain in front of the king and his courtiers. Now these horses could gallop across the sea as well as on land, and they were faster than the winds of March itself. The Sons of Turenn watched and took careful note. As the chariot came round for a second time, Iuchar and Iucharba seized the horses' heads, Brian took the charioteer by the foot and flung him out over the rail, and they all leapt into the chariot and drove away. Such was the swiftness of their driving that they were out of sight ere the king and his men knew what had happened. And thus ended the fourth quest of the Sons of Turenn.

For the fifth quest, they hoped to get the seven swine that could be killed and eaten every night yet be there again the following morning. For this they had to journey far, to the court of Asal, king of the Golden Pillars. But by now, the whole world knew that three young heroes from Éireann were plundering the kings of the world of their treasures in payment of a mighty blood fine; and when they arrived at the Land of the Golden Pillars they found it well guarded, with a watch kept by day and night, so that no-one who looked like they might be the Sons of Turenn should enter.

Yet a wise king always wants to learn the reasons behind every event, and Asal himself came down to the shore to speak with the heroes about their great deeds and why they had done them. Then Brian told him the story of the mighty eric that had been laid upon them, and what they had done and suffered so far in fulfilling it.

'And now it's my seven swine you want, is it?' enquired the king. 'And just how do you propose to get them?'

'With your goodwill, if we can,' replied Brian. 'And, for that, you will get our thanks and our loyalty on any occasion when you may have need of us. But if you will not grant us the swine, without which we will never be quit of our obligation, then we'll just have to take them by force.'

King Asal discussed this with his counsellors and they agreed that the Sons of Turenn should be given the swine, partly because of their cruel burden of obligation, but also because they would certainly be able to take them by force, given their previous achievements. So the pigs were given freely, and the Sons of

Turenn rejoiced because this was the first time they had won the treasure without trickery and bloodshed, and they vowed to honour the name of Asal forever for his compassion and generosity. And this was the fifth quest of the Sons of Turenn.

'And where do you go now?' said Asal as they sat talking in peace and friendship by the shore.

'Iorroway is next,' replied Brian, 'for the hound's whelp.'

'I'll go along with you,' said Asal, 'for my daughter is married to the king there, and maybe I can use some persuasion on him.'

So off with all of them to the kingdom of Iorroway, but here too the coast was strongly guarded and they were not allowed to enter. Then Asal revealed himself and was allowed to enter on account of being the king's father-in-law. He lost no time in telling the whole story, but it didn't work on the king of Iorroway.

The pigs were given freely to the Sons of Turenn and they rejoiced.

'Aren't you the fool to come asking?' snapped that monarch. 'No three heroes, however brave, are going to get my hound, whether in favour or by fight.'

Try as Asal might, he could get no further with him, and so he went back to tell this to his new friends.

'Oh, if that's the way of it,' said Brian, seizing the magic spear and the pigskin (for you know how young men are always ready to get into a fight, never thinking that they themselves might get hurt, and it's only when they get older that they learn sense). Brian and his brothers rushed up to the palace and a hard fight of it they had. Many times the three were separated, until at last Brian overpowered the king and brought him, tightly bound, to the harbour where Asal was waiting.

'There is your son-in-law for you,' Brian said, 'and I swear it would have been easier to kill him than to bring him all the way down here.'

'You've got the best of it,' said Asal. 'Now hold him to ransom and get your hound whelp.'

So the people of Iorroway gave the hound to the Sons of Turenn as a ransom, and the king was released, and with joyful hearts the Sons of Turenn went on their way. Thus was the sixth of their quests fulfilled.

Now Lugh Lámh Fada had, of course, been wanting to know how the Sons of Turenn were faring, and whether they had got any of the items that would be so useful to him if the Fomorians came back. And by divination he discovered how well they had got on, and that only the last two – the fairies' cooking spit and the three shouts upon the hill – remained. So, because there was still vengeance in his heart for the death of his father, Lugh used his druidic skills to cast a spell of forgetfulness on the Sons of Turenn. The next morning, therefore, they forgot all about the work left to do and developed a yearning to return to their native land. So they bade the *Wave Sweeper* bear them home with their treasures.

'Now,' they exulted, 'surely we are quit of our debt and will live happily, having won great fame for our deeds.'

When they landed in Éireann they wept for joy and kissed the ground, before journeying to Ben Eadar where the High King and Lugh were holding a great assembly. And they brought out one treasure after another and laid them before the High King and Lugh.

'Is the debt now paid in full, Lugh, son of Cian?' asked Brian.

'It's a good display,' said Lugh, 'but it is not lawful to give a quittance for an eric that is not complete. Where is the cooking spit from the Island of Finchory? And have ye given the three shouts upon the Hill of Mochaen?'

At this the Sons of Turenn fell to the ground and were speechless awhile from grief and dismay. Then, with heavy steps, they went home to see their father and sister, and on the morrow went down once more to the place of embarkation. For they realised

Lugh used his druidic skills to cast a spell of forgetfulness on the Sons of Turenn.

267

Ocean-nymphs lived in glittering palaces among the sea-flowers, embroidering fine cloths with gold and jewels, and singing in voices like silver bells.

that they had truly been caught in the net of fate, and while they had been telling themselves they were heroes and victors, all the time they had been but arrows in the hands of the gods.

Putting forth in their magic boat, they searched for a quarter of a year but never could get tidings of the Island of Finchory. At last Brian recalled that Lugh had said it was not to be found on land or sea. He made a magical water-dress with a helmet of clear crystal and plunged into the depths of the ocean. He searched for a fortnight until he found that strange island, where ocean-nymphs lived in glittering palaces among the sea-flowers, embroidering fine cloths with gold and jewels, and singing in voices like silver bells. They gazed upon him as he entered their great hall and seized a spit that was made of beaten gold. As he turned to leave, the nymphs laughed.

'You are a bold man, Brian,' said one, 'and you may take the spit for your daring, for we would never have granted it to you if you had asked.'

And, to tell the truth, I think those girls were admiring such a fine fellow, because they didn't see so many of them down there. Indeed they might have asked him to stay, and this story would have a different ending entirely, but they knew that he was on a quest of honour and so they didn't waste their time.

Brian took the spit and rose to the surface of the ocean, and his brothers lifted him on board. And thus ended the quest for the seventh portion of the eric of Cian.

Now the Sons of Turenn began to hope they might discharge their debt of honour at last. They set sail for the land of Loughlann, where the Hill of Mochaen was to be found. When they arrived, Mochaen himself came out to meet them with his three sons, Corc and Conn and Hugh – and four mighty warriors they were, father and sons.

'What seek ye here?' asked Mochaen. And they told him that it had been laid upon them to give three shouts upon the hill.

'And it has been laid on me,' said Mochaen, drawing his sword, 'to prevent that very thing.'

And then the seven men began to fight. Long and dreadful was that battle, and the grass was red before they were done. In the end, Mochaen and all his sons lay dead, and the Sons of Turenn lay over them, very close to death themselves.

But Brian opened his eyes. 'Brothers, do you yet live?' he asked.

'We are so near death,' they answered, 'let us go in peace.'

But Brian rose to his feet and lifted up his brothers while their life blood streamed down, and together they gave three hoarse shouts on the Hill of Mochaen. And thus was the last of their fearsome obligations fulfilled.

Then, slowly and painfully, they bound up their wounds and made their way to the boat, bidding it to steer for Ireland, in the hope that they could see it once more before they died. *Wave*

Sweeper took them to Éireann's shore and then swiftly overland, to the home of Turenn, their father.

'Go now to Lugh at Tara,' said Brian to his father, 'and give him the cooking spit, and tell him, too, that the last obligation was fulfilled on the Hill of Mochaen. Beg from him the magical pigskin, for if it is laid upon us soon, we shall recover.'

And Turenn went with all speed to Tara, gave Lugh the golden spit, and begged for the life of his sons.

Lugh sat silent for a while. 'They have accomplished wonderful deeds,' he said, 'and it is not fitting that they should live on. Far better that they die a hero's death, and that the bards and story-tellers of Éireann tell of their glories as long as this land endures.'

Then Turenn bowed his white head and went sorrowfully back to impart to his sons what Lugh had said. And, with that, the Sons of Turenn kissed each other, and the breath of life departed from them, and they died. And Turenn spread his arms out over the three of them and died also, for his heart was broken in him; and Eithne his daughter buried them in one grave. And thus ended the Quest of the Sons of Turenn.

And, with that, the Sons of Turenn
kissed each other, and the breath of life
departed from them.

The Second:
The Fate of the Sons of Usna

Now it happened that in the time when Conor Mac Nessa was High King of Ulster and his Red Branch Knights were famed throughout the land, that one night he and his chief druid, Cathbad, were bidden to a feast at the home of Felim. Felim's wife was with child, but nevertheless, she saw to the needs of their honoured guests, looking to the table and serving the wine as was fitting on such occasions. When she was leaving the hall, however, the child within her cried aloud. This startled the king, and he asked Cathbad to interpret such a phenomenon. Laying his hand on Felim's wife, Cathbad prophesied that the child would be a girl of surpassing beauty, who would cause bloodshed and anger and division among the people of Ireland, and whose story would live for all time.

'Better she be slain then, as soon as she is born,' suggested several of the king's nobles. 'That way, we can avoid all the trouble she will bring.'

'Not so,' said Conor Mac Nessa. 'If she is to be as beautiful as all that, then mine she will be, and mine alone.'

And when the baby girl was born, he had her brought to a separate fortress in the woods within the grounds of his palace and raised by foster parents until she was old enough to become his wife.

No-one was allowed to see the girl, and even the windows that faced towards Conor's palace were shuttered so she couldn't see anyone either. The only other person who had access (apart from Conor himself, who came from time to time to see how his protégée was progressing) was an old woman called Levarcham who was an expert in the *glam dichen*, or satiric verse, and thus could not be barred from any place for fear of the wrathful poems she might compose.

And so Deirdre – for that is what she was called – grew to become the most beautiful of women, tall as a young tree, slim as a wand, with long, golden hair, eyes as blue as the summer seas, and cheeks the delicate pink of the wild rose. Well-loved she was, but lonely enough, for all the company she had was her foster parents and the bitter-tongued Levarcham. Conor Mac Nessa she didn't think much of when he visited, since he was old enough to be her father and more.

One day, though, in the depth of winter, she looked out from the top of the fortress to where her foster father was skinning a calf on the snow below. A raven hopped down and began to sip the blood.

'Do you know,' she said to Levarcham, who was keeping an eye on her, according to the king's wishes, 'I could love a man like that – hair black as the raven, skin white as the snow, and lips red as blood.'

'Could you now?' said Levarcham. 'And where did you get an idea like that? For I'm thinking you have someone in mind.'

Deirdre looked guilty, and the old woman soon had it out of her. There was a side window in the fortress that looked out over the grounds where the Red Branch Knights did their training. The shutter had been broken at one time and a heavy curtain put over it, but Deirdre had discovered this one gap and had peeped out. Of course if she looked once, she looked again – and thus it was that she saw Naoise, the finest and tallest of the Sons of Usna (although his two brothers, Ardal and Ainnle, weren't far behind him in good looks and courage).

Now Levarcham knew well that any contact with young men was forbidden, but she had a soft heart underneath that bitter exterior, and so she arranged to let Deirdre slip out one day when she knew Naoise would be passing by.

Of course the inevitable happened. Deirdre was already in love, and Naoise wasn't long following her.

'Take me away from here,' she begged him. 'I don't want to marry an old man. I only want to be with you.'

Naoise was troubled, because his loyalty was to King Conor, but Deirdre's beauty was such that he couldn't think of anything but her. He told his two brothers, Ardal and Ainnle, and they agreed to go with him and protect Deirdre from the retribution that must surely follow.

'I could love a man like that — hair black as the raven, skin white as the snow, and lips red as blood.'

And so Deirdre ran away with the three Sons of Usna, and great was Conor Mac Nessa's fury. He pursued them the length and breadth of Ireland, until at last the four fugitives fled to Scotland where they lived a simple life in the forests and were happy.

Now Fergus Mac Roy, a great warrior and loyal friend to King Conor, thought it was a shame that the brave Sons of Usna should be thus exiled, and he argued with the king, saying that they should be pardoned and allowed to come home.

'It's an idea,' said Conor. But in his heart, anger still burned blackly and soon he worked out how he could gain revenge on the Sons of Usna and recapture his bride for himself. He told Fergus to go to Scotland and offer safe conduct and a pardon to the fugitives, and to bring them back under his own protection to the court at Emain Macha. Fergus departed on his journey to the coast, happy to see the young men coming home, but as soon as he was gone, Conor sought out another of his nobles, who lived not far from the coast where the exiles would land.

Deirdre and the Sons of Usna fled across the sea to Scotland.

'When you see them coming up from the shore,' he instructed this loyal servant, 'rush out and invite Fergus to a feast. Not the others, just Fergus.' Conor knew that Fergus was under a *geasa*, or obligation, never to refuse an invitation to a feast.

Deirdre was very unwilling to leave the safety of their happy life in Scotland, but the Sons of Usna were delighted. Trained as Red Branch Knights, they yearned to return to their fighting comrades, and so they persuaded her that going back was the best thing to do. When they reached the shores of Ireland once more, though, Conor's man was waiting with the invitation for Fergus, and he could not refuse.

'So we have to go on to Emain Macha without the protection of Fergus?' asked Deirdre.

'Don't worry,' Naoise assured her. 'Conor will not, in honour, lift a finger against us.'

Deirdre knew better, but they wouldn't hear of delaying and set out immediately, bringing her with them. Deirdre's heart told her that they were all riding into treachery.

Of course as soon as they reached Emain Macha, the three young men were surrounded and held at the mercy of the king's soldiers, while Deirdre, her hands bound, was dragged to the king's side on the royal platform and made to watch all that was about to happen.

Knowing they were to die, Naoise and his brothers made one last request: that they should perish together, so none of them would see a brother's death. This was granted, but it was a difficult task for the king to find anyone willing to put them to death. One by one, his Red Branch Knights, who had, after all, been the sworn comrades of the Sons of Usna, refused the request. In the end, it was Eoghan of Duracht who accepted. Without further ado, he picked up his sword and struck off their three heads with one blow.

At this, the agonised Deirdre uttered a shriek that echoed across the plains of Ulster. It recalled to Conor Mac Nessa, and indeed to his chief druid, Cathbad, memories of that night when the as-yet-unborn child had shrieked in its mother's womb, and they felt a deep foreboding.

As they should have done. For, angry at the way in which he had been tricked into abandoning his protection for Deirdre and the Sons of Usna, Fergus Mac Roy took all his men and left Ulster for the kingdom of Connacht, thereafter pledging himself to Queen Maeve, Conor's rival. He did not do this with joy, and indeed great was his agony of mind at leaving his native Ulster; but his king had broken confidence with him, and he had no choice in honour but to go. And that is how Fergus Mac Roy and his men came to be fighting on the side of Connacht in the great battle of the Táin Bó Cúailnge. And this departure was the beginning of the end for Conor's reign too, since a high king should never break faith or go back on his word.

When the three brothers had been buried in one grave, Conor took Deirdre by force as his queen. He assigned to her the finest rooms in his royal palace and gave her everything that a woman

When the three brothers had been buried in one grave, Conor took Deirdre by force as his queen.

could desire, from soft beds to silk hangings, rich jewels to fine foods, warm embroidered cloaks to intricately wrought gold torques. Nothing could soften her despair, stem her tears, or cause her to raise her head from her knees.

'Sweeter to me was the simple life with Naoise in the forests of Alba,' she wept. 'Joy it was to send him on his way to a day's hunting, and wait his return with eagerness at evening.'

A year went by in this way and at last, finding that possessing a woman by force wasn't at all the same as having a loving wife, the king came to her in desperation. 'Deirdre, is there anything I can give you that will cause you to look kindly upon me?'

'Nothing,' she made answer, 'unless you restore to me the warmth and the laughter and the love of Naoise, and that you can never do.'

This angered the king and he asked another question: 'Is there anyone that you hate as much as me, Deirdre?'

'Yes,' she answered listlessly. 'Eoghan of Duracht, who struck the fateful blow on the man I loved and will love till the day I die.'

'Very well, then,' hissed the king. 'I will give you to Eoghan now for a year, and you can see how you like that!'

The very next morning a fine chariot was brought round and Deirdre was placed in it, her arms bound for fear that she might escape. Conor stood one side of her and Eoghan the other, both of them smiling confidently at the way they could handle women as they drove away over the plains of Emain Macha towards Eoghan's fort.

'Aren't you a fine sight now, Deirdre,' mocked Conor Mac Nessa, 'standing up there like a tame ewe between two good rams!'

Deirdre made no answer but looked steadfastly ahead until she saw a turn in the road where great rocks rose out of the ground. In one moment, she threw herself backwards from the chariot and dashed her head against those cruel stones. In horror, the king stopped the chariot and lifted her up, but blessedly her spirit had gone to join Naoise at last.

Deirdre was buried with great honour, as befitting a queen, but secretly by night some of those who had loved her as well as the Sons of Usna came and took her body and buried it by the side of Naoise. A tree grew from Deirdre's grave and one from Naoise's; and as time went by, the two saplings twined together so that they were one tree forevermore, and could not be separated.

A tree grew from Deirdre's grave and one from Naoise's; and as time went by, the two saplings twined together.

The Third and Last:
The Enchantment of the Children of Lir

Once upon a time, when the Tuatha Dé Danann ruled Ireland, Lir was a great king, second only to the High King himself, Bodb Dearg. And it so happened that Bodb Dearg, in recognition of Lir's great strength and loyalty, offered his friend one of his two beautiful daughters in marriage. Lir fell straight away in love with Aobh, the eldest, and took her to wife; but it is said by those who were there that the second daughter, Aoife, had fallen in love with this splendid fair-haired warrior herself and was deeply jealous in her heart that her sister had won him.

Time passed, and Aobh and Lir were happy indeed, living in their castle on the Field of the White Hill. First she bore to him twin children, a girl and a boy, whom they named Fionnuala and Aodh, and then twin children again, both boys, Fiachra and Conn. Now they felt that their happiness was complete, and the place was full of love and laughter, the sound of children's voices and the whispering of the wind across the green fields. A pure white pony each of the children had, and a white hound too, to follow them as they rode abroad and were greeted by the people on their father's land, who loved them as much as their parents did. And so the four Children of Lir grew strong and beautiful until all spoke of them as wondrous indeed.

But then grief came upon the house of Lir when Aobh sickened and died within three days for all that they could do for her. Those were sorrowful times. Lir for many days and nights would talk to no-one and see no-one outside his palace, and his only comfort was the sight of his four loving children. Together they mourned, and gradually the love of his children eased Lir's aching heart.

It was then that Bodb Dearg sent word to Lir. 'It is not good for you to live without a wife to comfort you,' he said. 'I therefore offer you my second daughter, Aoife, as your wife. She is most willing for this, and I think it will be good for you also.'

At first, of course, Lir would not think of it, as it seemed like betraying his great love for Aobh, but at last he considered that Aoife could be a second mother to his children, whom he knew to be lonely too. And so he journeyed to the court of the High King and married Aoife, who was joyful that at last she had achieved her heart's desire.

But as is so often the case with those who get their heart's desire, it was not enough. Aoife became jealous of Lir's great love for his four children.

'They mean more to him than I do,' she thought to herself. 'See, he has their beds placed close to his own room, so that he can see them last thing at night and first thing in the morning. Surely I should be first in his affections!'

And the more she thought about it, the darker and stronger her resolve became to do away with them. 'Then Lir will be mine and mine alone,' she reasoned.

And so it happened that one fine summer's morning she invited the four royal children to join her in a chariot ride to

Drawing a druidic wand from her cloak,
Aoife struck the children one by one and
turned them into four beautiful white swans.

the shores of Lough Derravaragh to hear the birds sing and see
the flowers growing. Fionnuala's heart misgave her when Aoife
issued this invitation, and something told her not to trust her
stepmother; but her brothers were eager for the chariot ride,
and so she swallowed her suspicions and went along.

'Why not bathe in the cool water while you are here?' suggested
Aoife when they arrived at Lough Derravaragh. 'It is such a lovely
day, you will enjoy it.'

Soon all four children were splashing in the water, and, while
the charioteer was out of sight attending to the horses, Aoife
revealed her true intent. Drawing a druidic wand from her cloak,
she struck them one by one and turned them into four beautiful
white swans.

'Live now,' she cried triumphantly, 'three hundred years on
Lough Derravaragh, three hundred years on the Sea of Moyle,
and three hundred years at Irrus Domnann in the Western Seas.
And I say to you that a princess of the South must marry a prince
of the North before you spend one night on dry land again.'

And then she left them and returned to the palace, joy in her
heart at achieving her desire. Can you imagine the terror and
bewilderment of these four young royal children, hitherto accus-
tomed to a happy, carefree life among those who loved and pro-

tected them? Now turned into wild swans, condemned to suffer for nine hundred years on cold, unfriendly waters? At first they wept, and then Fionnuala put her wings around her brothers, Aodh, Fiachra and Conn, and vowed that she would hold them together and somehow they would all survive to the end of this dreadful enchantment.

In the meantime, Lir saw in surprise that Aoife had come home alone, and asked where his children were. She said they had run away because they did not love him. Lir knew in his heart that this could not be true, and went instead to her chariot driver to learn where they had been that day. The charioteer took him to Lough Derravaragh, where he saw the four beautiful swans floating and singing in piercingly sweet voices. Happily their voices had been left to them so they could not only sing, but converse with humans as well. It was thus that Lir learned of the treachery of Aoife, and his heart was sick indeed, for he knew he could not undo what had been done.

'If you may not come onto dry land,' he said, 'then we shall come and make our court here by the lake, that you may not be without company.'

And that was what he did, moving his entire household to the shores of Derravaragh and staying there with the swan children, for he could not imagine life without them.

In the meantime, what of the wicked queen Aoife? Well, when Lir went back to his castle to make these arrangements, he approached his wife with feigned smiles and loving gestures, as if he suspected nothing. While she was thus happy and off guard, he asked a question. 'What, now, Aoife,' he whispered to

The swan children spent a happy enough three hundred years on Lough Derravaragh.

her, as if in jest, 'would be the thing that you would most fear and loathe in the whole world, I wonder?'

And she suspected nothing.

'For sure, a demon of the air,' she replied. These were ancient, horrible creatures, condemned to fly in torment for all eternity while seeking always to torment others. Upon hearing this, Lir whipped out his own druidic wand and struck Aoife with it.

'Go now,' he cried, 'and be a sky-demon for all time!'

And with that, the wicked queen was transformed into a hideous, black, screaming creature that soared up into the air and through the chimney and out into the wide world where she is flying yet, and will be to the end of life and time. And good enough for her.

The swan children spent a happy enough three hundred years on Lough Derravaragh, with Lir and his court on the shore to keep them company (although it was always grief to them that they could not run and play on the green grass, or ride their ponies as they used to do, nor sit by the fire in the great hall at evening with their beloved father).

At last, however, the time allotted to them at Derravaragh was up, and with much weeping they were forced to leave those they loved and fly to the cruel Sea of Moyle, which rages between Ireland and Scotland. Here they suffered many hardships in winter snow and ice, when often their feet and wings were frozen to the stones on which they clung together for safety. Many were the nights that Fionnuala stood trembling on a tiny rock with her wings wrapped around her three brothers, wondering all the while why this had happened to them, and what was to be their future. And only that the birds of the air and the fish of the sea helped them with food and encouragement (for all had heard of the wickedness of Aoife), it would have gone hard with them.

Grateful they were when that second three hundred years was over and they could leave this harsh place for the gentler west coast and the bay of Irrus Domnann.

'First,' said Fionnuala, 'let us fly over the home we loved so much, and the lake where our father shared our first exile.'

The time allotted to them at Derravaragh was up, and, with much weeping, they were forced to leave those they loved and fly to the cruel Sea of Moyle.

And so they beat their pure white wings and flew over Lough Derravaragh and the Field of the White Hill, to see if they could meet with their father once more. But now there were no fine walls, no mighty ramparts to be seen – only old, crumbling mounds and twisted thorn trees. Six hundred years had passed, and the Tuatha Dé Danann had left the living world to new invaders, retreating underground forever.

Weeping and desolate, the swan children left the scene of their childhood and flew to Irrus Domnann in the Western Seas. Here, because of their beautiful singing voices and their gift of speech, their fame spread across the land, and many came to see and praise them. And so the last three hundred years of their enchantment passed gently enough, though they never ceased to feel the pain of the spell that had cost them their childhood and their happy lives.

Now it happened, at the end of this time, that indeed a princess of the South married a prince of the North. And she too had heard of the wonderful swans and desired them above all things for her new household. Her husband, being still at that stage where he could refuse her nothing, immediately went to the western shore, where the swans could be seen floating on the sea and singing sweetly while crowds listened in rapture. When they came close enough, the prince swiftly threw chains around their necks and dragged them to land.

'Now I have you,' he said, 'and I will take you home to my wife.'

But the nine hundred years of enchantment were complete at last, and the moment the swans touched dry land, their swan guise fell from them and in their place were four aged, trembling figures, old beyond imagining. As the prince fell back in horror, and the people, who had rushed forward to prevent the abduction of their treasured swans, raised their hands in despair, Fionnuala summoned her strength one last time.

'The golden days have passed and our people have gone,' she said. 'The only thing for us to do is to lift our voices once more, to sing the praises of those who have been here in the past, so that all may know the greatness of the things they did.'

And so Fionnuala, Aodh, Fiachra and Conn stood in a circle with their arms upraised and they sang gloriously of the Tuatha Dé Danann and the deeds they had done and the goodness of their golden world. And people came from all around to stare and wonder and listen. And as they listened, they began to hear singing coming from every side, from the hills and the mountains and the skies themselves. Then a great brightness overspread their vision so that they could barely see – but many afterwards claimed that they thought they saw, dimly, as if in a dream, the hillsides open and a fair, bright host of shining figures come forth with their arms outstretched; and the four lost, lonely travellers, now beautiful young children once again, go joyfully to greet them.

And so the Children of Lir were welcomed back by their own people and taken to Tír na nÓg, the Land of Youth, where they still live happily ever after. But the sound of their singing remained with the people of Ireland, who treasure above all to this day the gifts of music and song.

There is a distant isle,
Around which sea-horses glisten:
A fair course against the
white-swelling surge ...

[from *The Voyage of Bran*, trans. Kuno Meyer]